HOW NOT TO START A BACKPACK COMPANY

Jason McCarthy
Founder of GORUCK

HOW NOT TO START A BACKPACK COMPANY.
Copyright © 2020 by Jason McCarthy

First Edition, 2020

Book design by Alex John Beck / IA.AJB LLC

AUTHOR'S NOTE: I have changed the names of some of the people and some of the places in my story.

All rights reserved. No part of this publication may be reproduced, distributed, or transmitted in any form or by any means, including photocopying, recording, or other electronic or mechanical methods, without the prior written permission of the publisher, except in the case of brief quotations embodied in critical reviews and certain other noncommercial uses permitted by copyright law. For permission requests, write to the publisher at the address below.

GORUCK
415 Pablo Ave #140
Jacksonville Beach, FL 32250
www.goruck.com
team@goruck.com

ISBN: 978-1-7354374-0-8

Printed in the United States of America.

for java

Introduction 1

The Summer Journal 39

I'm Not Going To Respond To This For A While   90
I Fucking Ruined My Own Birthday   117
A Beautiful Drive Through Angel Fire   173
I'm Never Going To Be Your Business Partner   197
Brian And Blake At The Pikes Peak Trailhead   229
Then I Gave Her The Signed Divorce Papers   257
Burning Money Every Single Day   315
And Then There Were Two   329
At The Bagdad Cafe   347

Epilogue 357

Introduction

The hero entrepreneur dares greatly, risks every dollar and more, is on the verge of bankruptcy but at the last second figures out how to turn it all around, building a hundred million dollar business out of nothing, against all odds. It's the American way, it's hugely inspiring, and we celebrate their successes, as we should. I love those stories.

I have my own entrepreneurial experience in this journey of building GORUCK from nothing to where we are now, over $100 million dollars later, but it was not some hero's journey. And it certainly didn't feel like one, and still doesn't. The Grim Reaper didn't just show up one day for a showdown. He was right there with us, riding shotgun everywhere we went. He knew right when things got hardest, and he knew how to present easier alternatives. I gave him plenty of ammunition and he used it wisely.

The hardest problems that came about from starting a business were dealing with the problems in my life that had nothing to do with the business. I was embarrassed by the mess that was my life, and I sought to hide it from any and everyone. I was transitioning out of the military, where I had served in Special Forces. My wife Emily, who I grew up with and who was the love of my life, was in the CIA. We had been married for four years but never lived together. We both underestimated the strain that wars on different continents had put on our lives and our marriage. We just kept telling ourselves that 2008 was going to be our year, and it was going to be perfect.

The reality we discovered in West Africa was that it wasn't perfect at all. I lasted three months at her house in Abidjan before crawling home, head in hands with an onslaught of depression and a stupid idea for GORUCK that would bleed our joint savings down to almost nothing before leaving me completely broke. I was crashing on a buddy's futon on the Lower East Side of Manhattan, overlooking a graveyard better suited to braving the cold winter than I was. He stayed up bartending most nights, and slept by day. I passed my time crippled by indecision. How many blankets do I want, should I make a pot of coffee? Should I watch a movie, or read a book? Should I email Emily? There was always an excuse to do nothing, at which I excelled.

In no time, I had gone from a Special Forces soldier, serving on the tip of the spear, to a guy with no job, no wife, no mission, and no future. I was in no position to start a company or to be running one, or to be doing anything that a productive member of society would find easy enough. Eating was a chore, so I lost twenty pounds I didn't have to lose. Luckily GORUCK was little more than a tax identification number at that time. And luckily things took so long to develop.

At some point in that cold NYC winter came the simple idea that GORUCK rucksacks should serve as a bridge between Baghdad and NYC, between the military and civilian worlds. To take Special Forces quality gear and make it simple and beautiful without sacrificing performance, or toughness. It's the Baghdad/NYC thing that would endure in our thinking.

What I did not admit, or know at that time, was that the bridge I was building was for myself, first and foremost. And that's where the entrepreneur's journey must begin: from within.

Transitioning out of the military was harder than I could have anticipated. Losing the love of my life was crippling. GORUCK became an accidental distraction that offered an illusion of control, and I was happy to accept that. So I slowly began to pour my determination into it, in the hopes of not failing yet again.

My audience first and foremost was Emily. We were separated but not yet divorced, in contact by necessity and by habit. And because we were fighting over our dog Java — over who would get to keep him and who wouldn't - he became the subtext of every conversation and every email we exchanged. Our friendship muddied the waters, but our marriage already felt like the greatest failure of my life. To her, I wanted to prove that I was worthy. To the world, I wanted to camouflage my shame. Love and marriage and a bunch of kids with her, and happily ever after — that was the dream. As a consolation prize, GORUCK would have to do, and it became my revenge.

The story you're about to read is messy, raw, and representative of my life back then. It's the beginning of a tale that now feels light years removed from that amount of struggle, and the violence wrought on civility. I was doing a little work for GR1's 10th Anniversary in 2020, and happened upon a journal I kept in 2010, the existence of which I had completely forgotten about. That was the catalyst for these pages, as all the emotions came rushing back, nerve endings dulled but not dead. The misspent hope, the longing for my past life, the uncertainty of the way ahead. The brutal force of a beautiful adventure that simply wasn't working as planned, and what those consequences felt like, mile after mile.

During the Summer of 2010, I was between years at Georgetown's McDonough School of Business, and I had this idea that driving to all 48 states would be a good idea. That to meet people, get into adventures, and try to sell our gear along the way would somehow work. This plan was meant to justify not doing an internship at a bank, a conclusion I was predisposed to believe in. On that front, it worked, and my escape was hatched.

We drove almost ten thousand miles, met people and got into adventures, and we took beautiful pictures all over America. Ten years removed, I had glorified the adventure and suppressed the difficulties. But a journal lives forever, as written. The sense that emerged for me upon rereading my words is just how precarious this whole thing was. Far more so than I ever would have admitted, or knew. The trip was inspirational and certainly unforgettable, but beautiful pictures became a testament to what a veneer can look like on anyone else's seemingly perfect life. The words in these pages peel back the veneer entirely.

My goal is not to romanticize the pain, and it's certainly not to deter anyone from chasing their dreams. I believe you can do anything you put your mind to in this world, now and forever. My motivation is to set the record straight and, in fact, to encourage others to dare greatly along the path of their passions. To risk everything for what you believe in most, to follow your dreams. But in my experience dreaming isn't enough, that's what usually gets left out of the inspirational posters in the office bathroom. The truth is that you have to figure out how to make your dreams come true, and it's really hard and it will test your mettle day after day, year after year as you learn to pick yourself up again and again.

And again.

High School tennis trip
1996
emily & jason

Abidjan

The Background Story - Emily

In the Fall of 2007, my team and I left a bloody hot war in Iraq and came back to clean mountain air at Fort Carson, Colorado. We traded the freedom to drive around with .50 cals mounted to our guntrucks for the freedom not to, with all the adjustments that entails.

Emily was posted to the US Embassy in tropical Abidjan, Côte d'Ivoire, West Africa in her first year of a three year posting. She had to miss my homecoming, but she made the 8,000 mile trip to Colorado a couple weeks later. We spent a long weekend together, in love and alive and reunited. We were used to this way of life, where everything goes perfectly on the weekend and then we both go back to work. This time, we reveled in the time together even more so, as our worst fears had not come true.

And then she went back to Abidjan. She called me from the Embassy most afternoons, usually at midnight or 1 AM her time when she had wrapped up her cable writing. We made small talk without the Damoclean sword of Iraq hanging over us, she gave me the latest updates on Java, we counted down the days till we would see each other again. It was comfortably familiar.

I had a month off for Christmas leave, which would be the most consecutive time we'd spent together since we'd been married years earlier. So, in the span of a few months I went from the Iraq War to Colorado, hung out there for a couple months, then flew through Paris to get to one of its former colonies in West Africa where the love of my life was living. This was supposed to feel like a vacation, and a reunion, but my wartime instincts were still fresh, and from the second I got off the plane they kicked in. Not in an overt way where you have your Special Forces team and your guntrucks and you know you're at war. More like, this whole country feels like a Star Wars bar scene, starting at the airport in the middle of the night. Who's who, what tribe are they in, are they looking at us just because we're white or because they're checking us out for some other reason.

I was trained to assume the worst, and I did.

Emily and I picked up almost where we left off, in this whirlwind of a life we had chosen. She had volunteered to surge to Afghanistan but because she was already fluent in French, they sent her to Africa instead. She called it the Wild, Wild West. Far from the flagpole of Langley, it was a huge embassy but a small footprint of diplomats and Case Officers. She was exposed to a lot and could stay busy 365 days a year, all day every day. So she did, and that became her routine.

A month is nothing. You slip in, you slip out. The important piece of this vacation, though, was that it was a test run. I was set to get out of the Army later in 2008, so the question became what was I going to do when I moved in, for good. How would it be when Em got a permanent roommate, when her daily life of meeting people all over town and then heading back to the Embassy to write those meetings up and send them back to Langley would involve me. We were already married, of course, but marriage is just a title, a commitment but not a plan for how you're going to actually make it work.

She adapted her schedule that winter, which was easy enough to do since there were a lot more parties than usual. 'Tis the season. We went to the Ambassador's house for the big American party full of diplomats, it was normal with tons of free booze and a welcomed African flare. We also saw Gadaffi and his entourage from Libya in a dying old hotel in Abidjan. He was wearing a white suit with a large green outline of the African continent on the lapel that said USA, standing for his dream of heading the new United States of Africa. It felt like a combination of fashion show and tribal dance to ward off evil spirits that could turn into an orgy at any time. We stayed vigilant from our seats in the back, white as God made us, wearing western formalwear. America is the wealthiest superpower on the planet. If you find yourself sitting at the very back of the party, at an otherwise empty table for ten, it's not a subtle point they're making. We leaned into a few of the tables around us, Em passed out some business cards, said merci a lot, and l'Ambassade des Etats Unis, and we left them to their dreams.

It felt like a great escape as we walked out. We skipped through the

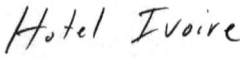

Hotel Ivoire

Halloween Party in Abidjan 2008
Smiling in costume

parking lot just to speed this whole thing up, and climbed into the car. Our diplomatic restraint was all gone by then so we burst into laughter, and it hasn't gotten any less weird all these years later. I still smile and shake my head when I think about Gaddafi and his entourage at the Hotel Ivoire — that we actually saw it with our own eyes.

Living that CIA lifestyle, we ate out almost every night, always with someone else of some importance. We heard a lot of stories about back home, wherever that was. Global politics is a game you learn to talk about. I learned when to and when not to talk about my time in Iraq. It was a lightning rod, especially for those from the Arab speaking world. No matter the country, people were sympathetic to the idea that soldiers don't get to choose where they're sent. And Johnny Walker Black makes every conversation a little bit easier.

By day, I had nothing to do. I hung out at the house, I tried to figure out what I was going to do with the rest of my life, what I was going to do when I moved here.

I was proud to be Emily's husband, but I also needed to find something to do. I could learn some French. But language school, that's a great thing to do a decade ago. What else?

I was bored one day and made Emily a "go-bag" for her car. When you drive around Abidjan, there are a lot of checkpoints. With orange diplomatic plates, you're allowed to drive right through them, but that doesn't mean you won't still get an AK-47 pointed in your face from time to time. And I had no read on the people walking around. It's a crowded, big city. The North is where the rebels are, the South is where the commerce is. They hate each other, violence is proof. How do you know when someone is going to start a coup d'etat? You don't. So in some sort of worst case scenario, Emily is out and about town and a coup starts and she can't immediately get back to the Embassy or to her house. I took an old Special Forces medical pack and filled it with things that might help her in that kind of a situation. This was second nature to me. When we would go out on missions in Iraq, we'd put a go-bag, or go-ruck in the trunk of the humvee. It would be full of extra bombs, batteries, ammunition, weapons, and water. The point was to have extra supplies in case you found yourself in an extended firefight. The concept was the same in Abidjan. Here's a bunch of stuff you want to have with you in case they start a coup downtown and you're isolated.

I showed her all the stuff in it, and said just leave it in the back of your truck. We talked about whether there was a market for me to do more stuff like this in Abidjan. It's a town where a nice dinner out costs twice what it would cost in Paris. And most of the population lives in poverty. The have-lots and the have-nots — there's not much of a middle class, or any middle class really. And the have-lots keep a pretty heightened security posture.

The people were scared to death of Java because the only people in town who can afford to have a dog, have a dog so they can protect their stuff. Dogs aren't pets, they're protectors. So the assumption is that every dog is vicious, even labs.

Did she have enough contacts of wealthy people who might want a Special Forces guy to help them beef up their readiness, their security at their house, to assess their patterns of life and determine if there was a better way to do it? Yes, she knew enough of those people. And with a little hustle from both of us, it could be a great way to meet people and gain access and placement into their lives. We thought it could work.

I made another go-ruck for the house, and put it in the guest room closet. I was showing her where it was, just in case, and I said this is pretty cool, I'm glad you have this now. "Jase, you should do the go-ruck thing" was what she said. She meant when I came back, I should do more of this. The security consulting company, just bring it to Abidjan.

That seemed a lot better than doing nothing. The way shipments overseas work is that diplomats are authorized diplomatic pouches. These are shipped directly to the Embassy and bypass all international shipping agencies. It's more secure, and postage from America is the same as domestic prices. I could leverage that service, but it was a grey area whether I could really scale a business that way — the short answer is that it's not for commercial purposes. Longer answer is that it would be a boon to her duties as a Case Officer.

We looped in her boss, he didn't have any problem with it, and thought it was a good opportunity. And out of the gates the quantities would be so small that it wouldn't really matter anyway. It seemed like it could work. The biggest question was whether we could just use pre-existing backpacks, or design our own. It would be better to just design our own so they're exactly what we want, I said. It'll save costs and can't be that hard. Famous last words, of course.

That trip to Abidjan in 2007 ended on a high note.

Trying to figure out how to run an import export business with Special Forces security consulting services in war-torn Africa so that my Case-Officer-wife could also gain greater access and placement to whomever I might meet, the diplomats and businessmen of importance in this part of the world. And while we're at it, we have to keep ourselves ready and prepared in case war broke out. It sounded fun.

We said our goodbyes and our I love yous. I gave her a big kiss with a big smile at the airport and told her I couldn't wait to finally live together. Ten more months, we said.

And away I went, back to Colorado.

That next weekend, my step-dad came to visit me in Colorado Springs. He stayed at the Antler's Hilton right downtown, and had a mountain view where you can see Pike's Peak on a clear day.

They had some hotel stationary, the big 8.5 x 11 size, and I sketched out a few ideas for what a "GORUCK rucksack" would look like. I went on LegalZoom and formed the company, GORUCK LLC, so that I could save receipts for costs I had no idea how to anticipate. I just knew that there would be costs, and you need a company to get tax breaks on those costs.

And that's how I officially became a business owner. A few conversations, a sketch, and an hour online filling out a few forms. Starting something is just that easy.

It was slow going. First off, I had a full-time job in Special Forces. We deployed to Europe and to Mauritania (West Africa) in 2008. That kept me busy, but I knew I needed to figure out as much as possible about how to run a business in Africa, while I was still in America. I didn't know the first thing about manufacturing, so I spent a lot of time researching it. That means, I googled stuff and watched YouTube videos. How are backpacks made? Stuff like that.

Eventually I found a designer who I hired to do some sketches. I thought he was going to be able to build the ruck, too, and get it scaled and shipped to Africa where I could fill it with supplies and sell it. He was just a designer, not a sewer or a builder. I visited him in Austin, where he lived, and felt good about the fact that I got to expense the trip. We stayed up late and refined the drawings, talked about the name and the story. We decided that the Velcro on the front, the patches would be 2x3, the golden ratio that's more beautiful to the eye. There is no uniform proportion on military uniforms. Some patches are smaller, some are bigger. 2x3 seemed perfect. Simpler design seemed better. It was progress.

I still didn't have a logo for the name GORUCK. Jack, my best friend from growing up, had been a male model and an actor in NYC for almost a decade. He knew all sorts of artists, and he found some old friends who believed in the whole idea for GORUCK, this storyline about Special Forces as the brand anchor. We went back and forth on what the logo could, would, and should look like. Should it have something distinctive inside of the word itself, G-O-R-U-C-K. Jack said absolutely not, we all came to agree.

What exactly should it look like though? I was in my team room one weekend, and I found the set of stencils that we used to identify our sealand containers out back behind the large boxes that we would ship all our team equipment to war in. I went out back with the spray paint and the set of stencils, and spray painted GORUCK onto a normal sheet of paper on the grass. I sent a picture to Jack and Tenzin, who had started a fashion magazine, and Tenzin took that and turned it into something far more

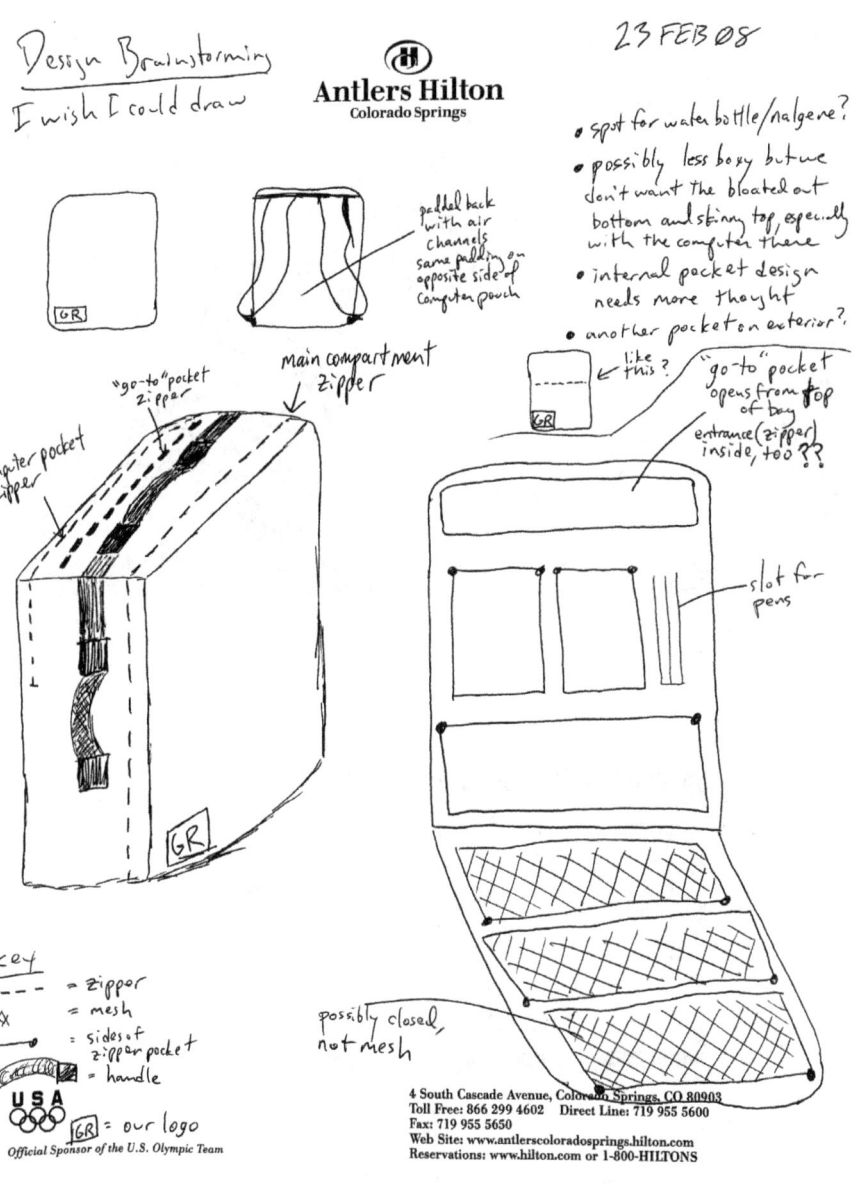

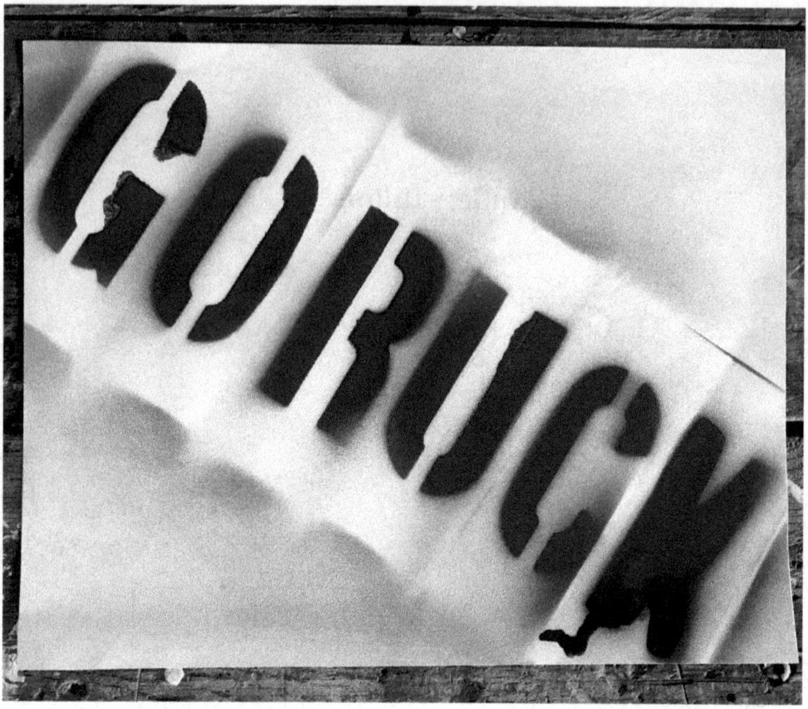
GORUCK

GORUCK
1.6
1
GORUCK

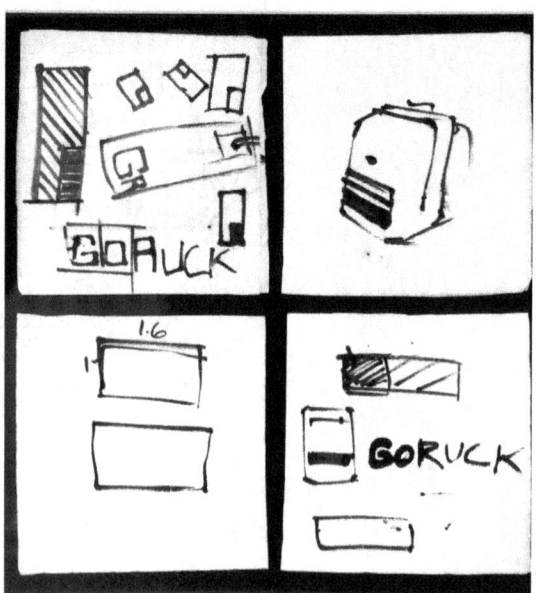

beautiful and simple, the font that we've used since that day. He also loved the reverse flag that I wore on my uniform, and did that logo, too. We could use it for patches and on our website.

That was the better part of a year's worth of work. The idea for a couple logos and a couple sketches. Zero progress on the actual building of the rucksacks. I started to realize I was just going to have to use pre-existing backpacks and get them sent over to Abidjan, along with supplies, to make that business work.

But the rest of the plan, the longer one – Em and I talked about that, too.

The idea that I would join her in the CIA. GORUCK would be a hobby, something to do over there. For her sake and mine, I needed a way to stay busy, and this would be that. The CIA would be our careers, hers and mine. She found out that I would have a greater likelihood for career advancement if I came in with a grad degree instead of just an undergrad one. So we talked about whether I should do that. If she transferred back to DC for a couple years after this post, I could go to school while she worked there. Then I'd go to the Farm, where they train you up to become a Case Officer, and we'd spend a few years in DC closer to our families, where we could also start our own family. My initial idea was to go to law school, but if it's all the same, and she said it was, business school is only two years, not three. Her boss in Abidjan had his MBA, and said that would work great. So that would save us a year. Sure, I'll get my MBA instead.

So I started studying for the GMAT, and was set to take it in the Fall of 2008, before I would leave for Abidjan. Em's boss also told her that there were more interesting stateside postings than at Langley, and that she should apply to more places than just HQ.

I took the GMAT, did pretty well, and started the application process for Stanford, Wharton, NYU, Harvard, Columbia, and Georgetown.

When I left the military officially, it was a lot harder than I anticipated. I cried on the drive from Colorado to Florida, where I was going to drop off all my stuff and then fill two big duffel bags to head to Africa to live with Emily. I had made some progress on GORUCK but would have to figure out more once I hit the ground. I had a few business school applications complete, and most importantly it felt like the end of a really long four years of war and deployments and now it was time to finally live with Emily.

To have a normal life together in Abidjan, that was the priority.

Back to Abidjan, September 2008

There was nothing normal about our time in Abidjan, all three months of it. It was weird from the get-go. Daily lives didn't go well with daily life. When you don't invest the time, when you try to skip to the end, when you are apart you grow apart. We didn't have much to talk about. She was trapped with me, and I was trapped in her house, with her. I learned quickly that my French was fine for bullshitting with someone at a cocktail party, but I couldn't have anything close to a conversation about security with anyone. Calling people on the phone to try to get the business was even more impossible. I could have looked for a local partner, a translator, but I was having enough difficulty speaking English with Emily. It was just really weird. The CIA had a counselor fly through. He met us at our house and sat in a government owned chair while we sat at opposite ends of a government owned couch. He talked about how we could essentially start over. How to take her life and put me in it. How to take my life and adapt it to where we were. How to fall in love again. He had platitudes about how marriages evolve, and have highs and lows and how that's normal. He didn't know us, and that one night was the only time I ever saw him. It didn't work.

Emily didn't have any real explanation for anything, and I didn't either. I ate very little and started drinking more. Tonic water with quinine was a leftover colonial staple promising to keep the mosquitos away. Goes great with gin and a lime, medicine on two fronts. Before too long, I didn't have anything to do all day because I didn't want to do anything. I stopped going to my French lessons, I hung out at the house and resented Emily for having so much work while I had nothing. While she's busting her ass for a mission we both believe in, I blamed her for my position in life. I thought of a million reasons why I was the victim. I made myself another gin and tonic, with a lime. She took me to diplomatic functions, I put a tie on and told myself she'd rather not have me there.

It happens fast. Both of our moms came over for Thanksgiving. They hung out at the house with me, we took a day trip to the beach, we ate at expensive restaurants with some of Emily's contacts, and she hosted a dinner party. We tried to pretend our lives were OK. Fake it till you make it, and we tried. Sort of.

I became wholly convinced that the more miserable my life was for her to see, she would shame herself into remembering how much we loved each other. That was my tactic, and the gin and tonics with a lime helped. Java didn't judge at all, and I loved him for it.

I lost a lot of weight, she cried a lot and so did I. We cried together, Java licked our cheeks.

And then I left Abidjan.

I sent a note to Jack, my buddy in NYC, asking if I could crash on his couch. Absolutely, he said. I told my family I needed to go back to the States to do some business school applications and work on some job stuff – it was all a lie. I was embarrassed and ashamed and didn't want to tell anyone what was going on in my life, which had felt almost perfect just a few months earlier. So full of hope, now vanished.

Video calls are a terrible way to work on a marriage. Emily and I chatted from time to time. At our best we were two old friends who knew each other really, really well. At our worst we were failing to make any part more than a friendship work, and the friendship became the problem. She couldn't talk to me, I had nothing to say to her that she wanted to hear. The only common ground was Java. How's he doing? He's good, he misses you. Stuff like that.

Time kept ticking on, and it was a cold winter in New York. Jack was a bartender at a tequila bar in the West Village called Tortilla Flats. He worked 3-4 nights a week. It was a 30 minute walk from his fourth story walk up apartment in the Lower East Side, on 1st between 1st and 2nd Avenues. Those walks were my only consistent exercise, to head across town so I could sit at the bar and drink free booze all night and pretend to be happy to everyone around. Jack became the only anchor in my life.

GORUCK had completely stalled.

Stanford and Wharton said no thanks to me as an MBA candidate. And I didn't have a job, or really even want one. I listened to depressing music like the Fleet Foxes singing about drops in the river. I read poetry like Prufrock, and even went so far as to memorize the whole Love Song. Jack spent most of the time at his girlfriend's apartment. Occasionally they'd try to get me out for something normal like dinner. I felt like the third wheel because I was, and my only comfort was escaping back to the apartment.

Occasionally, Emily and I would have a great conversation, things seemed to be getting back on track. In the wake of those, my productivity for anything beyond nothing improved greatly. I applied to a few more business schools. Once you've done one or two, it's largely a formality. And I placed an ad in Craigslist NYC for a "backpack designer." That felt like a big accomplishment. I got more than a few replies and found it easy this time to weed out those who could only draw vs. those who could actually build something. A couple living in Bozeman, Montana, sent a note with a link to their website. It detailed how the whole process would go, from start to finish. From legal contract to prototype samples. Real physical things.

They quoted me $4,017 for six samples. It seemed like a lot of money. I would later come to find out that it should have cost 10X that. Each sample is a day's work, once you know what you're building. Trish and Sky, the Wookeys, had recently been laid off from a bag company in New

Lower East Side
cemetery to my rear

Zealand, and Sky was trolling the Internet looking for any work he could find, including Craigslist NYC.

These are the kinds of things that you have no control over in life. It could have gone such a different way. I don't know what would have happened if they wouldn't have found me. Over the next several months, they drove the entire process. I looped Jack in to all of the back and forth. I would take pictures of the assault packs I had with me in NYC, and describe how they should be different. Simpler. Jack and I spent a lot of time discussing the MOLLE webbing. Was it too militaristic? What if there were less, just a few rows? Two rows? One row? We sketched the outline of the bag onto construction paper on the floor of his kitchen and drew on top of it to better see what it would look like, proportionally. We decided on 3 rows of MOLLE. It's just so functional, I said, it has to have some MOLLE. If we want it to thrive in Baghdad and NYC, we need to have it on there.

Baghdad and NYC had a nice ring to it. Special Forces has the best stuff, but it's out of place in NYC. Too much MOLLE, too many straps, too militarized. That doesn't matter so much in war, but when you want to blend into an urban environment, it's vital. Simpler is better, a classic military style has worked well in every generation. It's timeless and classic at its best, and that's our goal.

The first sample that the Wookeys mailed, they sent it to Jack's girlfriend's apartment above the smoothie shop on 2nd Avenue. I hated it, it was too soft, didn't feel tough enough. Had too much spacer mesh. But it already felt better than anything else out there if you were judging by the whole Baghdad NYC thing.

The next sample — we made it exclusively out of the tough 1000D Cordura, the same material used for all my Special Forces packs. No spacer mesh, nothing weak like that. We removed buckles you don't need. I told Trish and Sky that the standard had to be that you need to be able to drag it behind a humvee from Baghdad to Basra and it'll be fine. They laughed at me like I was crazy, but they also kind of got it.

Emily and I agreed to meet in Morocco, to try to see how we were feeling about each other a few months later. We stayed in Marrakesh, walked around the bazaars, bought carpets and paid our respects to Casablanca. The strawberries you could buy at the market were juicy, the views of the city from the rooftop of our hotel reminded me of Iraq, minus the promise of violence. It was kind of like traveling with a cousin, or a really good friend, except there's something hanging over the conversations. You know it and she knows it but you ignore it because if you talk about it, you'll ruin everything. It's no way to spend a vacation, or a life.

We had fun, but not that much fun. She had to get back to Abidjan, and I had decided to travel around a little bit after dropping her off at the

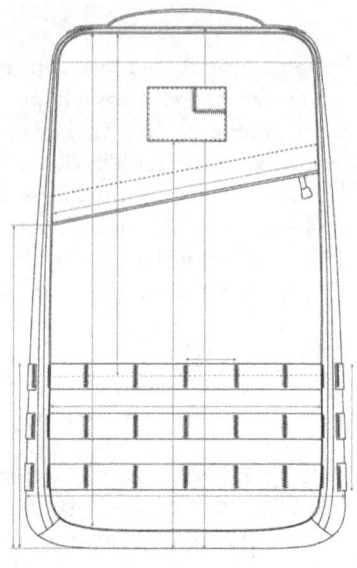

GR1 Line Drawings
Finished 2009 in
Bozeman, MT by Sky.
Always loved these
Simple & Beautiful

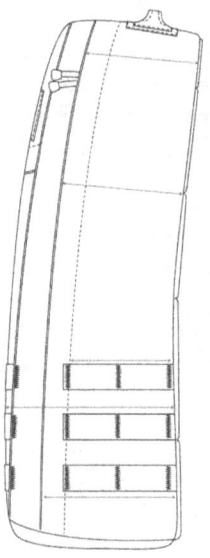
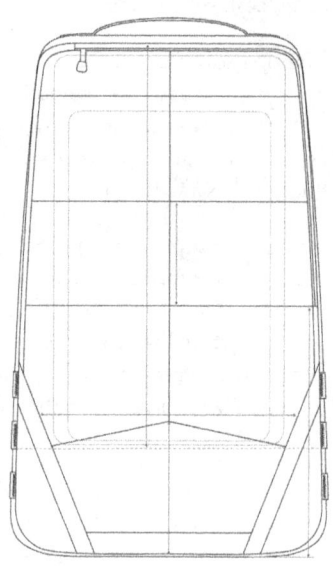

airport. Her flight was delayed, there was nothing to eat except for some paprika potato chips and snickers, and we bought both and sat at one of the tables at the airport in Marrakesh to prolong our goodbyes, and to avoid answering the most important questions.

My cell phone rang, it was a 202 number from DC. Who would be calling me now? Pick it up, she said. I hit silent because we only had a half hour left together, maybe for the rest of our lives.

How do you tell the girl you love that you love her? You just say it, and I did. And she said she loved me back. We both had tears in our eyes, sitting across from each other, and I regretted eating any of those paprika potato chips, they were churning acid in my stomach. We didn't really have much else to say so she got up like it was time to go. Might as well.

I hugged her goodbye and she hugged me right back, it was easy and natural. Then she grabbed her bag and walked toward the diplomatic security line.

She turned around to wave, to blow me a kiss. I blew her one back, and watched her disappear behind security before slouching down back in the chair, exhausted and distraught.

The paprika potato chips were open on the table. They were disgusting to look at, and to smell, so I threw them away and walked out of the airport, sick to my stomach. I took the train to Tangier, a town right on the Strait of Gibraltar across from Spain.

When I got there, I wanted to send Emily a note, that I was OK and that I loved her. I booked a room at the motel El Muniria, the same place where Burroughs had written Naked Lunch. Staying there was my best attempt to find some inspiration somehow for something, but I still needed Wifi to get about the business of daily life, and it was not to be found there.

I walked around and found a hotel with free access and opened my email to see a note from Georgetown University's McDonough School of Business. They had accepted my application, but there was also a note from the Associate Dean.

He said he had tried me the day before and could I please call him. I wondered if he called everyone who got admitted. I clicked on the acceptance and there was another explanation that I had received a scholarship called the Connelly Foundation Scholarship, good for full tuition to the school for both years of MBA study. I was confused because I hadn't applied for anything like that, why would they give that to me?

I forwarded the note to Emily and heard right back (she was at the Embassy) — Wow! That's amazing I'm so proud of you honey. She called me, it probably cost $3/minute, but she called me to congratulate me as I was sitting in the lobby of some hotel I wasn't staying at, in Tangier, Morocco, by myself. Yeah, it's great.

I packed up my stuff and walked around to think about it. I stumbled into the main square, bought a fruit smoothie, they had an option for one with an avocado mixed in. I thought that was crazy but in Abidjan, Emily had an avocado tree in the backyard and we ate them often, almost daily. Oui, avec l'avocat s'il vous plaît, I said.

It was an open square with plenty of trees but no leaves. People doing what they do all over the world in these kinds of places.

Across the way there was a phone booth. I bought a calling card from a street vendor and walked over, dialing the number the Associate Dean gave me to call him. His name was Jett Pihakis. I dialed a bunch of numbers before his, then got his assistant, then was put through.

...

"Dean Pihakis, this is Jason McCarthy."

"I assume you saw already?"

"Yes sir, I saw."

"Well, I wanted to congratulate you. There are only five of these scholarships we give out every year, and you earned yours and we hope to see you at Georgetown in the Fall."

It was an obvious yes, but I wasn't 100% sure.

"Yes sir, that sounds great. I love DC, my wife is in the State Department so it's a perfect fit for me to be back there."

"Excellent, let me know if I can be of any help at all."

...

I walked all over Tangier. What was I going to do with my life? Did I really even want to go back to school? Did I want to go back to DC? What if I just got on a plane now, back to Abidjan?

I told a few other people, it was unanimous that this is not the kind of thing you say no to, under any circumstances. I didn't know what I was going to do with the rest of my life, but a free MBA from Georgetown was a no brainer.

I accepted their offer, and the scholarship. And I was going to start business school in the Fall of 2009 at Georgetown University.

It wasn't GORUCK and it wasn't the CIA, but Emily would have to come back through DC at some point, so it would have to do.

Put a tie on to hide
the mess back home

Georgetown

It was a weird thing to start business school married, officially, but not tell anyone. If I hadn't gone to Georgetown, I would have been anywhere else not DC, where she was, and this all would have ended much faster. We even talked about that.

That summer, Emily and Java came back to the US, as anticipated. She was back for good, until they sent her somewhere else. All her household goods, everything from Africa, got sent to my apartment in DC. She had a hotel room just up the street, through the government. Java bounced back and forth between us. We were separated but talked about her moving into the other room in my apartment, she could pay rent, we could save money. Java wanted to see both of us, after all.

Java kept us talking. It was a custody issue. She couldn't take him to Langley, I took him to class a few times just to prove the point to her that I could take him anywhere. I'm a better parent, I thought, and she needs to realize that. He wasn't technically a service dog, but nobody brought it up. Better to beg forgiveness than ask permission. Java and I became inseparable. I rushed home all days, at the expense of anything at school, to be with Java. With him was the only place I felt at home anymore.

A few months into business school, the school hosted a formal at The Willard, a DC institution two blocks away from the White House. I thought more than I wanted to about not going but brought it up to Emily. She was also reluctant to go, but we decided maybe it would be good for us, or something like that. Alex, who is the editor of this book and a big part of the summer story in these pages, was in town from NYC (we can't remember why anymore) and I bought a ticket for him, too. He had spent weeks with us in Abidjan taking photos and witnessing our lives unwind firsthand. The three of us went together, two suits and a formal dress. Em looked stunning.

To everyone at school, I was the old Special Forces guy with a dog. Nobody knew about Emily. We decided to wear our wedding rings (more fake it till you make it) and I introduced her to a couple of friends as my wife Emily. I could feel their eyes get big, smiles and nice-to-meet-yous unable to camouflage their surprise.

Whispers circling, Emily and I were dancing like you're supposed to at these things. One of my classmates, a girl with short black hair and a thick Russian accent, cut in between us and pointedly asked me when we were going to go grab a drink. She's six inches from my face, with her back to Emily. I can still feel how big my eyes felt and I looked over her shoulder and right at Emily and then I told this girl I don't know, probably never. This is the kind of rudeness that offends every Southern sensibility Em has. Then Emily asked me with daggers, is there something going on here that I need to know about? No, I said. The only proof she needed was my dumbfounded face and the fifteen years she had spent learning all my tells.

OK, she said, satisfied with my answer. And then she turned to this other girl and let her have it. Who the hell do you think you are? is how that convo started and it evolved fast. The music didn't have to stop for the music to stop. I pulled Emily off the dance floor and we grabbed a cab out front before punches were thrown. Suffice it to say you probably don't want to cut in on anyone's dance like that, much less a couple in crash and burn, but especially not when the wife works at the CIA.

Java was excited to see us home early but our night was the casualty along with whatever hope was left for us. By all accounts, the night was a disaster.

That Monday Em went back to work and I went back to school and our lives began to unwind from each other, even faster now.

As you distance yourself, the coming back together becomes more complicated, and harder. You put aside the reasons, and you slip back into the emotion of the moment. I loved you and you loved me and this isn't working. You see each other, you both want the fucking dog, you start to resent the other person for wanting the fucking dog. And it only becomes about the fucking dog. Java loved us both without judgment, that was his gift in all of this.

Another night was especially excruciating. She was at her hotel, I was at my apartment. I went to get Java. We both said horribly painful things to each other, on the P street sidewalk, long after all but the vampires had bedded down for the night. She blamed me, I blamed her, for everything. We both blamed ourselves.

Then she said quietly, as you would to a long lost friend you hadn't seen in years, "You need him even more than I do. You can have him, Jase."

I gave her a hug and took Java home, back to my apartment, and cried myself to sleep into his shoulder.

February of 2010 she left for Florida. She had resigned from the CIA. She told me she was going to move to Brazil, that she would be happy there with someone she had met. That's not an easy thing to hear, and I started to wonder harder why we had failed, what I was lacking that some guy in Brazil had.

Business school continued. Java and I continued. Every day in the afternoon it was time for the creek, Java just wanted to get outside, and it turned out it was medicine for me, too. There was a lot less booze in my life, and more miles with Java by my side.

Business school is more of a gentleman's school than a rigorous test of academia. Most projects are done in groups, there's a lot of emphasis placed on networking your way to a successful internship between the two years. There is plenty of free time to do other stuff, whatever you want to do.

GORUCK was something to do.

Through the Wookeys, I found a factory in Commerce City, Colorado, close to the Denver Airport, who said they could build our rucks. I flew out to meet them, saw their factory, which we'll call the Colorado Bag Co. It was the first factory I had ever been in, so I guess it was fine. Great, let's do it. I found a friend of a friend who could build websites, and she was cheap. Great, let's do it.

A buddy in business school told me there was some new event, a mud run called Tough Mudder in early May. I should reach out and see about a partnership, there were lots of potential synergies between a Special Forces backpack and the "toughest one day endurance event on the planet" designed by British Special Forces. I sent a note through their website. I took the $20 bus up to NYC to meet with the Co-Founders, Will and Guy. Will loved the idea of me putting a team of Special Forces guys together to do their first event. So I was on the hook for that, and the timing was good, just as the business school year was finishing up.

GORUCK added a real world element to business school. Manufacturing and Operations, Marketing and Finance. I could relate everything from class back to the specifics of GORUCK, not just to the textbook.

I took Entrepreneurship in the Spring, and found out that you could have classmates work on your idea. I pitched GORUCK to the whole class on the first day, and it was the only idea that was more than just an idea. I found a few other people who were excited to work on a real business. Our task was to put together a business plan.

The idea of that seemed like a waste of time to me, but I figured it couldn't hurt. I bought pizza and beers once a week and had everyone over to my apartment, which was a lot cheaper than going out, and Java was literally right at home.

This whole setup reminded me of how you get things done in Special Forces, by creating force multipliers. Beer is currency, you make friends and influence others, you share your vision and get their buy in, you build rapport, and you maintain rapport by showing up and doing the work with them. One man can only do so much work, but if you bring beer and pizza and now you're working by, with, and through five other people, they become your friends and your force multipliers, they're working toward your mission success and you're a lot closer than you'd be if you went it alone. And the whole thing costs you $50/week.

Businesses you work on in business school are built on growth models. How can you scale, what's your plan to do that? I assumed GORUCK could be successful. The brand of Special Forces tied in with a rucksack. Baghdad/NYC. I didn't know anything about how to grow a business, though. You read case studies about advertising budgets and marketing campaigns.

That's great and all, but I don't even know where to start. Hire someone to do the campaign, then allocate the cash to spend on the campaign. I didn't have any money and didn't know how to get any for that, either. I don't even have any rucks yet, or a website. I don't know what anything costs, and I'm the only employee, and I'm paying for this job so far.

The retail model came to mind. Find a bunch of stores you can sell through, get more and let them sell more. These are the ideas that pizza and beer inspire. Sure, let's build that model out.

I asked Jack if he wanted to come down from NYC and help. He brought his albino Australian Shepherd named Asher (after Arthur Miller's middle name) to live with me and Java. He worked a few shifts a week at a BBQ spot on M Street called Old Glory — I never once went to drink with him there.

In the afternoons we took the dogs to Rock Creek Park, we talked about how to conquer the world through GORUCK. We made lists of stores, which basically works like this. Find brands you like, see where they're carried. Google GQ's best men's stores. Add those to the list, too. Then find other cool brands at those stores and see where they're carried. You can do this kind of planning forever.

The assumption is that these kinds of expensive cool kid stores can support higher price points, which we'll probably have since we're building in the USA. We still didn't have any costing on the rucks from the manufacturer in Colorado. But we have a list of stores.

We talked about how we could get them to carry our rucks. Well, we can cold call all day and mail samples out.

That sounds horrible, I thought.

==What if we just drive all over the country and just go from store to store to meet them face to face.==

That seems like it's more our style, old school. Jack thought it sounded great. As a test run, we both visited a small men's shop in DC, the kind we would be targeting, and showed the owner our samples. She wasn't in the least bit interested in carrying them, and told us as much. She was rude, we wrote her off.

The business plan continued until we wrapped it up. We turned it in to our professors with placeholder numbers on costs, which would eventually prove to be about $100 per unit too low. That's a ton, of course. It took me reviewing this plan ten years later to realize that we'd done that. Oops.

Our professors loved it. They were both angel investors and entrepreneurs in their other lives, the mystique of which is palpable when you're in business school and not those things. I think they fell more for our passion than our plan.

Here are some of the excerpts (of a 29 page document) that I find the most interesting, over a decade later. Handwritten comments are mine, from Brooklyn, NY, 2020.

GORUCK

Business Case

Jack Barley
Alex John Beck
Jason McCarthy

John Franklin
Michael Friedman
Lauren Foster
James Kopelman

It's humbling to think about how many good people played a role in GORUCK

Executive Summary & Business Description

GORUCK designs, manufactures and sells military grade gear directly to consumers online and is targeting select brick and mortar stores nationwide. GORUCK's branding as cool, adventurous, and military grade is critical to its success; therefore, initially, every effort will be made, even at the expense of sales volume in stores, to safeguard the brand. In its broadest sense, GORUCK targets modern adventure seekers.

[handwritten: Brand first]

According to our research, 93% of people own a backpack and 43% of those who own one use it at least twice a week. In other words, the market size is significant. Additionally, as businesses move towards more casual dress codes, more people are bringing a backpack to work, rather than a briefcase.

[handwritten: This will be easy. So easy.]

Research indicates that 68% of people say the quality of stitching, construction, and materials is 'very important' when buying a new backpack. People are willing to pay more for a better product. GORUCK gear is 100% military grade and designed for its functionality, durability, and unique style. The functionality and durability claims are justified by its association with the military, Jason's background in Special Forces, and the product launch at an adventure race called Tough Mudder, where a GORUCK team of ten will each complete the 'toughest one day adventure race on the planet' with a GORUCK bag full of bricks.

The unique style is subjective and best legitimized by controlling the stores GORUCK sells in and our online branding. GORUCK aims to be perceived as a preeminently 'cool' brand, as captured by the picture/holding page currently up on www.GORUCK.com

True to military roots, the GORUCK logo is a removable patch, allowing someone the ability to remove it and add their own or add nothing and leave our distinctive 2" x 3" Velcro exposed (picture below), in which case it becomes a default logo and another strong but subtle brand element associated with GORUCK. GORUCK aims to empower consumers to customize their GORUCK gear.

[handwritten: Can't believe we put 'cool' in there like that in quotes.]

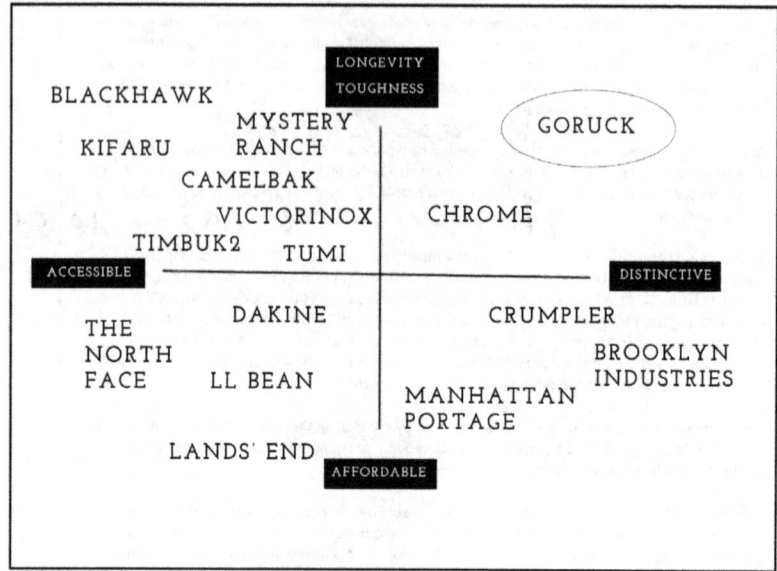

Competition

The chart below shows the clustering of competitive bags around GORUCK's three offerings. While this chart shows there is no correlation between cost and volume (in liters), it does show that the GORUCK bags, while not either the largest or the most expensive, are above average cost for their size.

I think the team got this exactly right.

The Team To Beat – Team GORUCK – US Special Forces Running With Rucksacks Full Of Bricks
Tough Mudder have agreed to let this team of former and active duty US Special Forces test out what they claim is the toughest rucksack on the planet (www.goruck.com) on May 2. To give everyone else a chance, they will be running with their bags stuffed with bricks. If you think you have what it takes to beat them, we suggest you email their CEO at jason@goruck.com.

Between May and September 2010, Jack Barley will visit approximately 400 stores in target markets to engage store owners and buyers. We plan to be discriminating in which stores we sell in, ensuring that the brand stays strong and that we sell in stores with salespersons/owners who engage customers and can explain the value of GORUCK products. In the East Coast market, urban and bike stores are our primary target; on the West Coast, outdoorsy stores factor in as well. Major chain stores and stores that cannot support our price points are not our focus because the customer service is limited and the brands are primarily sold by name recognition and price. Because the margins are lower in stores and volume of sales is not significant, retail store sales is more a branding tool than a serious revenue driver, at least initially.

Our target is to have GORUCK products in 50 stores across the county by the end of September 2010. The stores we choose will drive traffic to our website, where the margins are much more favorable and consumers can begin to appreciate how to 'customize' their own GORUCK gear with accessory pouches and patches.

Badass pic of my buddies made me miss that life. Instead, let's sell rucks. Didn't seem very important.

Estimated Operating Statement: Years 1-5

	Year 1	Year 2	Year 3	Year 4	Year 5
No. Stock Keeping Stores	64	74	84	94	100
Avg. Inventory Turn per Store	2.75	3.00	3.96	4.00	4.00
Avg. Units in Stock per Store	18.33	29.00	29.00	29.00	29.00
Avg. Wholesale Price	$ 31	$ 48	$ 45	$ 42	$ 39
Wholesale Sales (Units)	3,227	6,438	9,647	10,904	11,600
Wholesale Sales ($)	$ 107,186	$ 309,843	$ 476,505	$ 557,420	$ 593,000
Direct Sales (Units)	2,750	4,687	10,011	12,513	15,642
Direct Sales ($)	$ 267,263	$ 521,012	$ 1,110,955	$ 1,388,693	$ 1,735,867
Total Sales (Units)	5,977	11,125	19,657	23,417	27,242
Total Sales ($)	$ 374,449	$ 830,854	$ 1,587,460	$ 1,946,113	$ 2,328,867
Cost of Goods Sold	$ 149,987	$ 321,324	$ 544,030	$ 617,527	$ 675,066
Marketing Expenses	100,016	92,245	167,732	223,415	305,019
Operating Expenses	78,175	185,537	483,350	604,187	755,234
Total Expenses & COGS	328,178	599,106	1,195,112	1,445,129	1,735,319
Pre-Tax Profit (Loss)	46,271	231,748	392,347	500,984	593,548
Income Tax Liability (30%)	13,881	69,524	117,704	150,295	178,064
Profit (Loss) After Tax	32,390	162,224	274,643	350,689	415,483

Financial projections are based on a number of key objectives:

1. GORUCK products carried in 100 stores by Year 5.
2. The addition of at least four new primary bags and a full line of accessories by Year 3.
3. The successful rollout of the full-featured online store in Year 3 (Note: online sales will exist from Year 1, however the Year 3 update will be much more robust in scale, scope, and reach).

Forecasts for companies with zero revenue are fantasy. To grow faster, just assume more growth. That's not reality.

So we had a plan, blessed by Georgetown professors, believed in by our team. We just need to execute on it now, I guess.

That was my thought process.

<u>Brand Building</u>

Business school doesn't make you a businessman, and I had no understanding of our numbers. When we finally got the costing for the rucks, it was a punch to the face. They cost about what I had hoped to charge. My bank account was empty, I couldn't cover the costs for any first run of bags.

I called my step-dad Mike, who I had kept in the loop on GORUCK since the very beginning. He knew about the Tough Mudder event, about the summer road trip plan, he had reviewed the business plan we had turned into my professor. He told me I needed some operating capital, "cash is oxygen for any business," he said, and said he'd partner with me and give me $150K for 20% of the company.

Family, Friends, and Fools — that's who you're supposed to raise your first capital from. Mike, by my account, was all three. I took his offer, which was harder than I expected because I felt like I had done something wrong by not being able to self-finance. His cash allowed me to place some purchase orders for $75K from our manufacturer in Colorado. By his math, GORUCK was worth $750K at that time, with no revenue whatsoever. I didn't know how he did that valuation, and I didn't really care. All we had was an idea and some samples and a mud run coming up, and the loose outline of a brand with Special Forces roots selling rucks that would thrive in Baghdad and NYC.

He later told me he figured he would lose his money, but wanted to support his son. As of 2020, he's our Chief Operating Officer. But don't let me jump ahead, this is the prequel.

The goals for the Summer of 2010 were to build a brand and start the sales process to build a business. When it comes to building a brand, I was a big believer that GORUCK had no brand without associating with other brands. Meaning, if you've never heard of something, it means nothing to you.

Nobody had ever heard of GORUCK, so we had to build a brand on the backs of other brands. It made me uncomfortable, but I had to leverage my past in Special Forces. Marketing? That sounded like a four letter sell-out kind of word. No thanks. But brand building, I was OK with that.

The American Summer — yup, America is a great brand, let's co-brand with America for sure. And is there anything more American than summer? The manufacturing was all in the USA, too, so that was an easy message. US Special Forces Founder building tough gear that thrives in Baghdad and NYC, made in the USA and driving all over America blogging about how great America is, and doing all that as we approach stores to carry us. They'll practically beg us to put us in their stores, we thought.

Jack's job was sales, so he'd be driving separately (yes, we thought that was a good idea) so he could focus on that.

I'd be in the 'GORUCK Truck' with Java and we'd bring along two old friends as well, Alex and Sara, so we could focus on the story of the summer. Alex had a background in fashion and in adventure travel photography and we had lived together for a year before I joined the Army. Sara had a background in sales at Lilly Pulitzer and was Jack's girlfriend all throughout high school. We were all good friends.

GORUCK, America, Special Forces, Java, and a bunch of friends hitting the open roads.

Let's do it, and it'll start May 2, 2010.

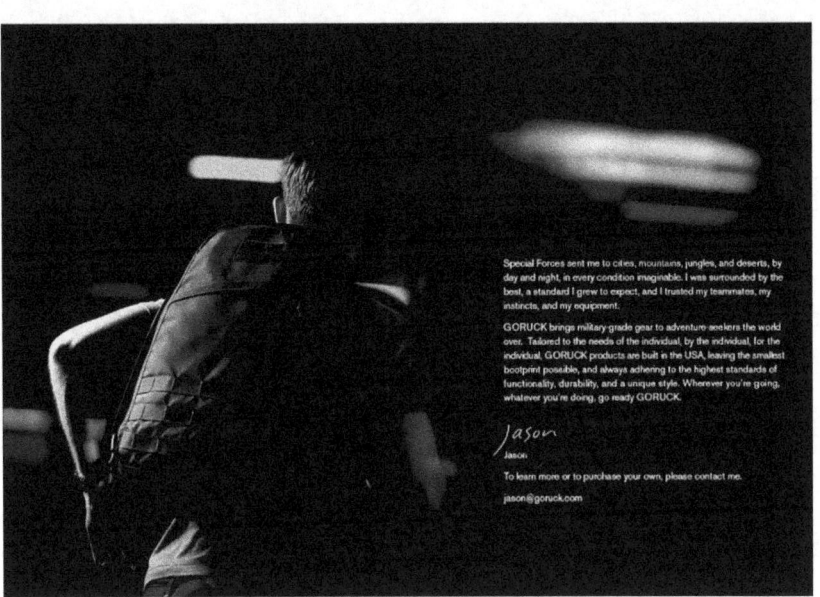

Our first website — the landing page at goruck.com

We couldn't process payments, you had to email me directly, which nobody did ☺

The Summer Journal

My private journal from the road, as written in 2010.

Plus select emails.

It gets more interesting as everything (and I mean everything) starts to fall apart.

This is intentionally long, unedited, raw, and uncut.

All the buzzwords.

Java's pillow — one of the straps we ripped out.

April 30th, 2010

100 rucks showed up to my apartment in Georgetown, DC.

We needed to take them to Tough Mudder and sell them. Jack and I pulled them out one by one. We started pulling on the shoulder straps and all the stress points.

I pulled a little harder and heard stitching pop where the straps attach to the rest of the ruck. I pulled a lot harder and the shoulder strap came out. This was not what I was hoping for. Failure before the big hero's parade.

We had no choice but to thoroughly inspect every single ruck to see if they were all like this. The test we performed was that we put the ruck on the ground, back panel facing up. We put our shoe between the shoulder straps and pulled as hard as we could on the straps. If we heard any kind of popping at the seams, we rejected it.

10 rucks passed, 90 failed. Insult to injury was that we had to go buy tape at the 7-Eleven and package the boxes back up, and take them to the post office a mile away, and wait in line to mail them back. A mild form of torture unto itself.

I called the owner of our factory and told her that if any of these had been given to my buddies going to Afghanistan, they could have died because of this kind of equipment failure.

April 30; May 1 & 2 / Tough Mudder

The guys showed up to my place in DC with beer and brats in tow, charcoal and stories from every corner of the world.

Now that I'm out of the Army, I love catching up with my guys who have new stories of adventure I wish I could have shared.

No time like whenever you can to catch up with old friends.

May 1 / The drive to Bear Creek, Pennsylvania from DC.

10 of us doing Tough Mudder. 7 Green Berets. Team GORUCK, team to beat, and it's actually almost here.

The race prep Saturday night May 1 got us in shape for it all in our own style. We were camping out on the course. Three kegs, a fire pit, and clear skies. The night looked very promising.

Bear Creek said 'no fire'. Since I used to ski there as a kid I felt especially slighted. Not a problem, we'll start it up once you're long tucked into your beds.

Just FYI, ATV's start with pocket knives, I recommend Benchmade. Course reconnaissance the night before big race day. We knew the layout pretty well by the end of the night's festivities, racing up and down the ski runs. The stealth fire kept us entertained back at GORUCK Central. We had made some new friends over the course of the day who made it our way that night to see what was going on and watch some Ranger TV with us.

If you were up at 2am, you may have heard Corey screaming an ode to joy at the top of his lungs from the top of the highest mountain. Pretty sure there were some golf carts after us. Presumably Bear Creek security? Can't be sure, though. They never caught us.

Wake up came fast once the night faded out.

Tent setup in the vendor village, Murphy's law struck so we had no power. Home-made cookies for breakfast, we all loaded our GR1's with a stack of bricks.

Since it was our product launch and everything, I guess I was a little nervous in a different way than with most races, but also more excited. There is a pre-Tough Mudder and post-Tough Mudder arc to the GR story. Thanks to Will and Guy (the founders) for letting us do it our way.

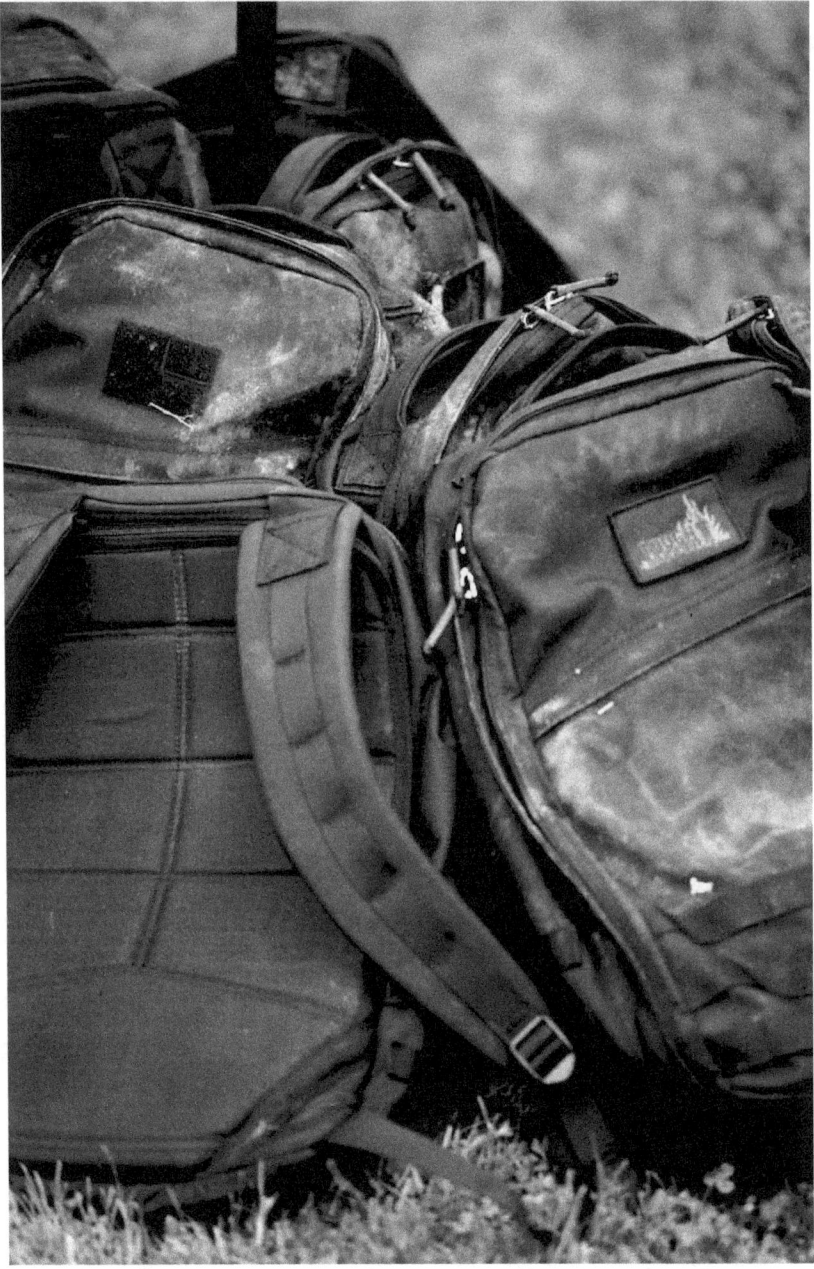

The course itself was good old-fashioned fun. Infinitely more so as a team - it reminded me of a lot of the obstacle courses my fellow candidates and I plowed through together in Special Forces training. And it came, and it went. Nothing was perfect but we're off and doing it with the people we have, the friends we've made, and the places we visit. This is literally the beginning.

NOW LET'S HIT THE ROAD

Jack and Jason, Java and Ashe

To cure a hangover, just add bricks to your morning mud run

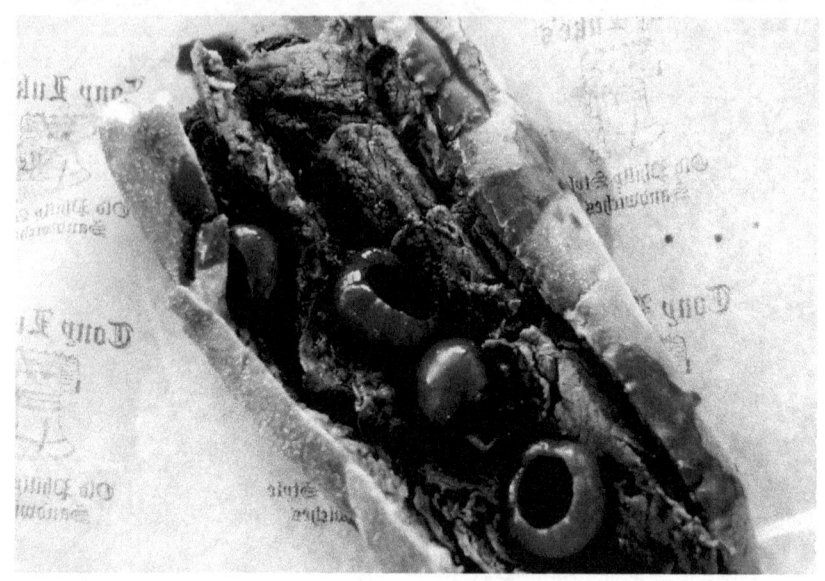

May 4 / Philadelphia

Tony Luke's

It seems so cliché to ask where the best Philly cheesesteak in Philly is. A buddy of mine named Tony, appropriately, offered up Tony Luke's without any hint that there was somewhere else in its league. It was the wrong direction for us from where we were in Old City, but heading in a straight line is usually boring.

Tony Luke's was worth the foray into seeking out authenticity as a tourist, a feeling I disdain but am more comfortable smiling through as time goes on. The location is 'sou-philly', not far from the ballpark, under an elevated Interstate 95. The patrons are solid and diverse but all seem like they live and work in Philly. Cops meet Phillies fans meet a random bunch of guys in suits, all there for the same reason. You can watch the magic through a glass window as you wait in line, action in the kitchen seems a constant, and even though they're all probably at the point where they don't want to eat their own restaurant's food anymore, you'd guess that they still really love and have a lot of pride in the place. They should, it's a city landmark in its own right.

Phillies Cardinals was in the air, lines that seemed very common were well established. Some guy walked into the place with a Cards jersey on and the sharks were circling. Guys eating in their cars right out front with big smiles. Cheese wiz if you want it, I don't know if I overstepped purity laws with peppers and hot sauce on mine, but even if I did, it was incredible.

May 5 / Tortilla Flats, Cinco de Mayo NYC

What the hell is Cinco de Mayo anyway? At TF's, it's loud and excessive, and plenty cheesy, streamers hanging from the ceiling, pictures cover nearly every square inch of what I assume is a muted paint job that hasn't seen the light since 1982, back when TF's opened. The staff, though generally tired of the customers from yesterday on, must appreciate that Cinco de Mayo fell on a Wednesday this year, giving them one more good night of tips this week.

We showed up at 9 to meet some old friends we've known since high school, the type of friends though that are easy to stay in touch with since they're in NYC (and may always be).

Jack showed up a bit later than the rest and looked right at home here, though his bartending days are over. Any place you work for seven years must feel like the house you grew up in. Even when it's sold and someone else lives there with their pictures on the wall, you still own the memories it gave you and the right to see it now for what it was, so there's always part of it that's yours. Actually several of our friends have worked at TF's over the years, all of whom grew jaded by routine but who still vaguely remember from time to time that it's a really cool place to stop by.

==Nostalgia runs deep once in a while, even for the good in a relationship killed by how bad it became.== And I had a great time with a packed bar of strangers and old friends.

Coronas led to Patron and a much later walk back to the East Village than I expected. Thankfully the sidewalks never roll up here, I guess - part of the social fabric that keeps everyone out later than common sense would dictate.

May 7, 2010 (wee hours) / Burlington, VT

3am is always an interesting time to introduce yourself, especially after staring at yellow lines in the dark the whole night. Let's just say the town mayor was not there to greet us, nor was the welcoming party, but we got a sense of things with the pups in tow. We walked around Church St and the main square.

I guess I wished the town were still a bit awake beyond casual packs of excess stumbling about with no clear purpose, but I reclined my seat and slept off my disappointment pretty easily after the long drive. Lake Champlain is the western limit, well worth the short walk on any perfect morning as ours was. If you ask Java, he'll tell you it's not to be missed, even when it's 50 degrees warm.

Java and Ashe got the insider's tour of the Lake and unexpectedly the Magic Hat Brewery, which has to be the coolest brewery ever for letting us take our dogs in and tour the place. Ben and Jerry's factory, also just up the road, was a little less so but the kids loved all the ridiculous moooooooo-ing that the guide must be forced to do, so it's tough to argue with that.

May 7 - May 8 / White Mountains, NH Friday

Campfires are my favorite show on TV. Campfires with the dogs and my best friend in a gorgeous national forest are even better.

We rolled into our spot off the Kancamagus Highway at dusk and gathered enough wood to grill some hot dogs for us and the pups, and to keep us entertained while we drank some local brews, made friends with our neighbors, and crawled into our bags to catch up on sleep.

Thank you, New Hampshire. For slowing it down for us, for the national forest that rendered my cell phone worthless, for great beers and better scenery, for the chance to take it all in. Live Free or Die.

May 8 / Portland, ME / $13 Lobster sandwich.

When in Maine, lobster sandwich. No matter how many travel books I have and how fast my Internet connection is, local advice is golden.

Solicited local recommendations for the best lobster spot in a trite and cliché kind of way (meaning with a smile) but it was worth it and I didn't care. Their answers all led us to Gilbert's on the waterfront. Chips were average, beer was no better no worse than usual, but the $13 Lobster sandwich and Heather's service - she's taking the Foreign Service Exam, hope she passes - were both casual and hit the spot. The perfect prequel to walking around Portland happy with its small town feel. The rain didn't matter, but I was glad I had my rain jacket, content cruising and talking to the locals.

Checked out a couple shops - tons of waterproof stuff, fishing-themed. Biggest agenda item was asking the locals whether we should try a different lobster spot for dinner.

DRAFT BEERS
BROOKLYN LAGER
$4.00
$4.50
$5.00
the Scürvy Dög
BBC

Angela

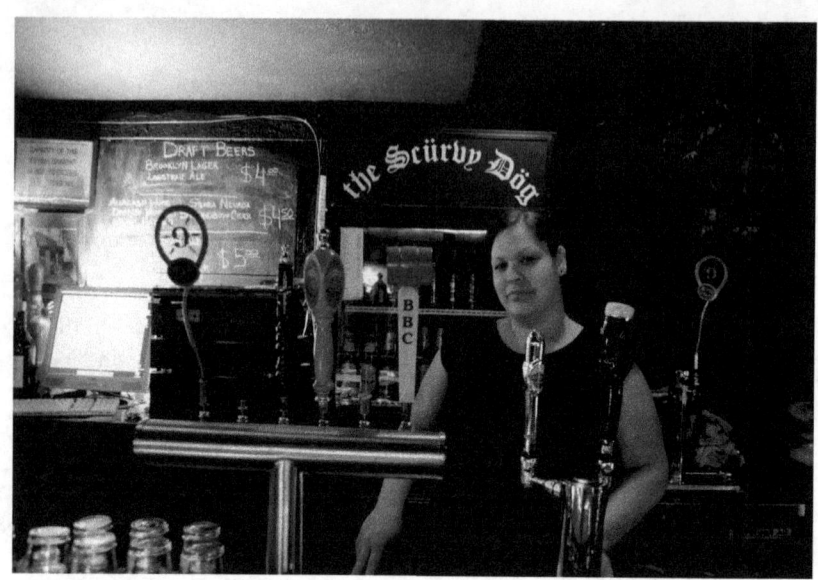

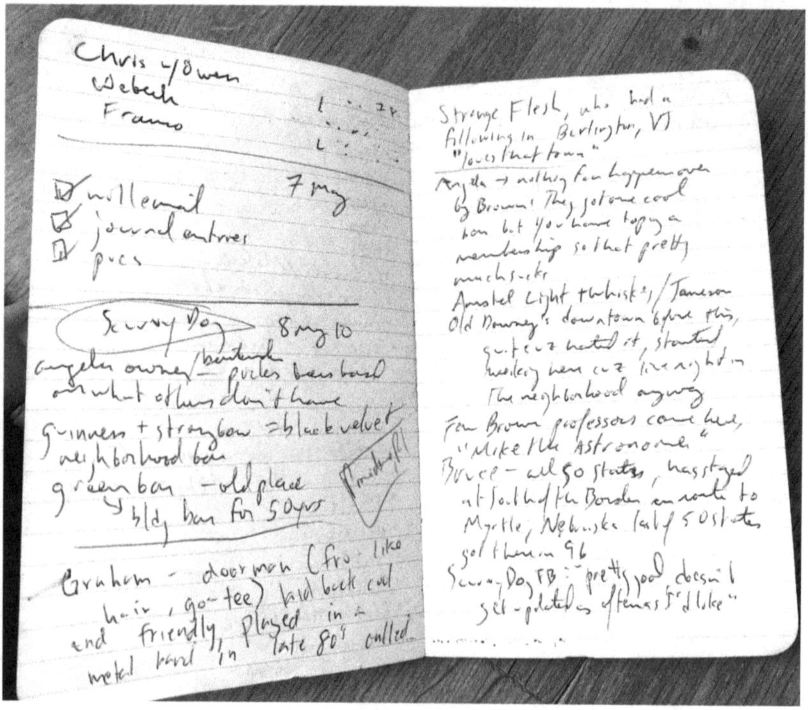
Chris w/Owen
Webech
Franno
7 my
mollemail
journal entries
pics
Scurvy Dog 8 my 10
angela owner/bartender – picks beers based on what others don't have
guinness + strongbow = black velvet
neighborhood bar
green bar – old place
bldg bar for 50 yrs
Graham – doorman (fro-like hair, go-tee) laid back cool and friendly, played in a metal band in late 80's called
Strange Flesh, who had a following in Burlington, VT
"loves that town"
Amstel Light + whiskey / Jameson
Old Downey's downtown before this,
the neighborhood anyway
Few Brown professors come here,
"Mike the Astronomer"
Bruce – all 50 states, has stayed at South of the Border en route to Myrtle, Nebraska last of 50 states
got there in 96
Scurvy Dog FB: "pretty good doesn't get updated as often as I'd like"

May 8 - 9 / Providence, RI

Without any agenda we rolled into town and parked around Brown University. The only tips we had been given were Italian restaurants found up on the State Hill part of town. Allegedly there are a few mobsters running around who eat really well up there. I always feel so removed from the Godfather when I imagine that anything similar at all actually still happens.

Brown was pretty. And staid other than a game of cricket on the lawn. To their credit, these guys looked like they grew up with it and knew what they were doing. But nobody who even attempts cricket didn't grow up with it, so what the hell do I know anyway? I have no idea how it works so I can relate to Europeans puzzled by American football. But while Java and Ashe would have happily joined the game, I wanted to break out of a Brown world played on green grass.

Up at State Hill, there was some guy sitting out on a lawn chair, apparently checking people out - but not IDs - to decide who to let in. He had a white tank top and flip flops on with a gold chain and flowing chest hair, so I don't think he was judging on jean labels for posterity's sake. We should have gone over to have a chat, or at least tried to, but I just wasn't feeling it. Leaving the pups in the car up there. Downtown was packed, nowhere to park and all in all it seemed a bit trite everywhere, like a crowd at a Miley Cyrus cyrus concert is supposed to look. I was a bit jaded at this point, though, so take it for what it's worth.

An old buddy hit me up with a rec - The Scurvy Dog - off the beaten path and certainly the type of place you would drive right past and never think twice about going in. For anything. In fact, even when we got there, I didn't want to go in. Its proximity to the interstate and lack of signage made it practically invisible, perhaps only an outline around a clear nothing. But.

Usually being the only one in a bar at 8pm is depressing, one rung below drinking at home with Java. But Scurvy Dog doesn't have the vibe like nobody will show up. It felt like the people just weren't there yet. So we chatted up Angela, the owner bartender, about the place. It used to be a drug dealers' mecca known as the Green Bar until July two summers ago. That all changed once they started checking ID at the door since, in her words, criminals don't carry ID.

Graham was our laid-back doorman. Besides the present, his 15 minutes came from singing in a metal band in the 80's called Strange Flesh. I guess it had a hell of a following in Burlington, VT. Now you know where to find him.

one pool table
no short stick

Angela wasn't ready for her drink yet, which we offered, but instead continued to drink her Dunkin Donuts iced coffee. What the hell is it with DD in this part of the country? I thought Starbucks was taking over the world. I did not order a red velvet, a very popular drink here, which is Guinness and Strongbow, but instead opted for the Long Trail Triple Bag without knowing anything about the double bag. It was a little sweet, as advertised, but still a strong beer. One is enough.

Angela prides herself in her beer selection meant to avoid crossovers from other bars in town. It's about as unpretentious as it gets in here. One pool table. Always the right answer for a bar. A missing short stick since it walked out months ago. Elvis, black chalkboards, tape decks and records. One shitty TV in the corner. And charm everywhere, but more than anywhere from Angela. When you come, you can drink some beers you won't find elsewhere without a lot of effort, but she's also got that one she called the local PBR.

Everything is better in a tall boy. That's how the Brits got them in Iraq and passed them along to us.

The place slowly filled up with the young and the old accustomed to each other - well beyond the type of tolerance exhibited when some Rockefeller type brings a tattooed cousin to the private country club. Graham 20 years ago hangs with Graham now just fine. And vice versa. And the local PhD who's been around the world on academia's great searches was comfortable chatting all about American mathematics in the 1600's.

It's the kind of place where Angela drinks her DD iced coffee, stocks the bar, watches me and Jack play a lousy game of pool with no short stick, and won't let us buy her a drink till she's good and ready. The only thing you might not guess is what she would let you buy her.

May 9 / Boston, MA

Nostalgia for the summers of my youth in Cincinnati watching the Reds dictates that I will always love going to the ballpark. Any ballpark. For any game. I am always there with my father. And my fielder's glove. I am always there to eat hot dogs and watch him drink beer. Even when I'm the one drinking it now, he's the one who's really enjoying it.

My fondest memory of Fenway growing up was the story about Yaz's game winner against the Reds in (1975)? But the Sox only won that game. The Big Red Machine took it in 7. But Fenway is a legend, always will be. Which is why the name remains on the place, which I guess is why they upgraded instead of built new from scratch. So that the cynics of the world couldn't cry foul ball.

It still feels to me like a remake of a less consumer-driven time, though now it's trying to force $50 worth of snacks on you. Upgrade it and they will still come, businesses, too - come they do, especially to see the Yanks. It got me excited. But signs meant to feel like the 1950's never do. Billboards all over everything, including the updated Green Monster - feel tacky, and make me never want to put my money in Bank of America.

But Jack just loved it, for me I guess it never could live up to how I used to watch it on my grandfather's 12" TV. My father enjoyed the beers I drank, the Fenway dog was fantastic. I will always love seeing fathers and sons at the ballpark together because those are some of my fondest memories as a kid. But I'm getting older. I find myself talking about the good old days.

The game was surreal from the upper right field bleachers. We were higher up than the Green Monster, which just didn't do it justice. We had to go lower to make things right. We snuck in below and my father enjoyed another beer. At one point we heard random cheering from the fans, the ushers were leading someone out. A diehard Sox fan laughed by yelling and told anyone who could hear that that was the kind of cheering that could only come from Red Sox fans watching a Yanks fan get thrown out. A sense of pride in his team, his city, all Sox fans, the passion was contagious. **I should try to stay young and realize these are in fact the good old days I will be talking about with my family some day.** And so my father had another beer. And smiled.

May 11 / Colorado Bag Co / Overnight to Denver

MANUFACTURING PROBLEMS

Heading out to see Fey and Colorado Bag Co. Anyone who ever told you that dealing with factories was a nightmare can find a sympathetic ear with me. If it's not one thing it's another. Then back to the one. We are trying to create an iconic brand, so my tolerance for mistakes wears thin. The bags look pretty good, they're perpetually the 98% solution. But the 2% floats and it eats up all of my time right now.

Prototypes look great, production run comes out different. Forget this, forget that. A lack of attention to detail will get you killed is how I was trained, so a nice little reroute from BOS - ATL - DEN and I'll be there to Quality Control (QC) everything, even as I look hard for alternate suppliers.

I need my 650 bags I paid for based on prototypes that simply don't replicate themselves. Just when I thought I could focus on the other stuff. Fey's been the brunt of my rage over the last few months, one hour-long corrective powerpoint presentation at a time. I am hoping to help her fix her side of the house to get me my bags and hats. We are already selling to stores and have a Details magazine story coming out in Aug/September. Time will fly by to get there. Each day seems like a week with all that goes on but feels like an hour long race by the end of the day when I wonder where the hell all the hours went.

I love my few minutes in the morning with Java, just the two of us. I love it all. All the problems, all the challenges, I've always felt guilty about the easy path. Even now I feel like I should be off somewhere making a difference, the mountains of Afghanistan have long fascinated me. Since September 2001 anyway.

But I'll run GORUCK for a while until something greater calls me. I know that the fork leads elsewhere.

Till then, my focus is on making the perfect bags and trusting the power of our story to somehow make a difference wherever the highways of America take me.

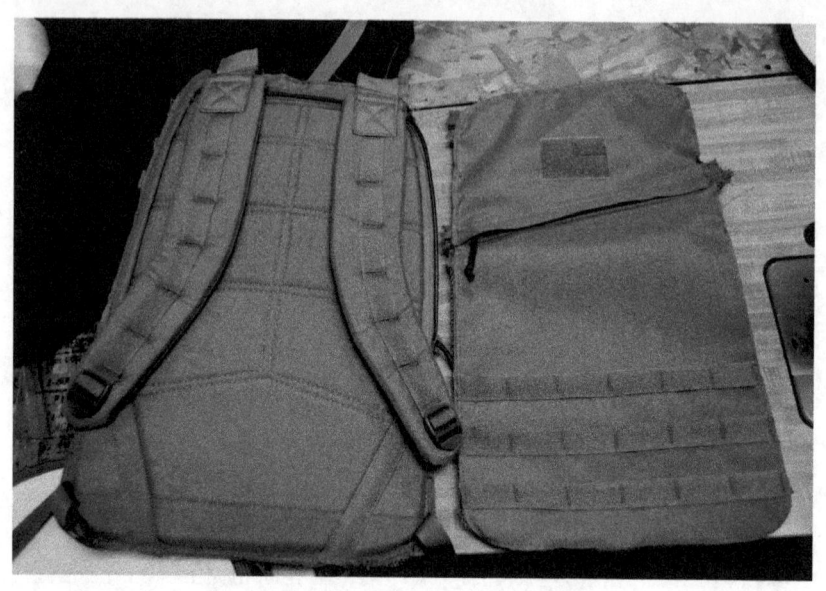

May 12 / Denver, Colorado / Colorado Bag Co then back to NYC

Quality Control is the hardest part of this whole process. Face-to-face time out at Colorado Bag Co has me optimistically pessimistic about their ability to deliver the products we need. Short days that should have been longer but for the hours they keep.

"How do you feel about all of this?" Fey asked. Well, I'm five months into this with you ladies and I don't have bags yet. I have no doubt you can make me one or two but can you make me 650 and then 6,500? I have my doubts, so the proof will be in the products. Don't mess it up again.

I have to train them to my standard. Not out of some self-grandeur but rather out of a respect for Special Forces and my own word to the people who will depend on our bags. Military grade is sort of like facts, subject to interpretation. I am ultimately responsible for it, so I hung with all the QC-ers, giving them my thoughts on what mattered. And why. I sent a few back to be fixed. I've been told the most humiliating thing a sewer can do is tear apart his or her work. The better the sewer, the harder it is to do. But the goal is so that they don't have to fix anything anymore. Fey inspects one bag personally per batch. Ship smaller quantities. And repair everything to my specs.

I like them and understand that the process of making our bags is very intense. Watching these ladies have to manhandle the subcomponents under their various sewing machines shed light for me on the process and just how difficult it is, how 'imperfections' are going to be part of the character of each bag, but that our gear is worth what we are asking. Good luck to anyone who wants to make a knock off.

Jessie

May 13 / New York City Again

Wee hours. Jack hammered at Tortilla Flats, drinking free beer till he starts bitching at me about money.

I took the bus in from LGA so he could have some time with Jessie. His idea that he expected me to have paid for his bills came out of left field. Drunk and griping about money is not a good idea. Went back to Jessie's confused to where he was. Near fight after he told me he was going to knock me the fuck out. Nose to nose. Go for it you drunken fuck and see what happens. I was neither comfortable with this rage, nor in the mood to sit down and take the high road.

I left, took Java, almost hit the road to ESPN. Have a nice summer dick head. Slept in the car instead. Took his bullshit texts and emails.

Woke to a flat tire. You have to be kidding me. Texted Jack and he met me with French toast at the gas station on 2nd and Houston.

Some people can blow up and forget. Other people besides me I guess. Jack and I are brothers, so we can have these fights and get over it. We joked about GORUCK dissolving, which never would have happened, and hit the road for ESPN.

From: Jason McCarthy <██████████████████>
Date: Thu, May 13, 2010 at 4:58 PM
Subject: Press release

To: Alex <██████████████████>

>> aj -- I've been working on a larger press release for places like Selvedge Yard that want more info on us and the Summer. I mostly like the first two sections, but don't like the 'Inspiration' section yet, pasted below.

>> I'm thinking of scrapping it altogether even though JP at Selvedge was very curious about it.

> INSPIRATION - GORUCK is a truly American brand and its products all share in common three benchmarks for excellence that set them apart: superior functionality, durability, and a unique style. GORUCK identifies with and has taken inspiration from many places. Its commitment to durability and functionality come directly from Jason's experience in the US Special Forces, a truly American institution, which sends its operators into hostile environments with the best equipment on the market and where individualization of both gear and their thinking is essential. Other overtly American brands GORUCK identifies with are Ford, Harley Davidson, Levi's 501, and Ray Ban. Each of these brands has broken down the walls of its specific market to attain a truly iconic status by creating a better, simpler product that transcended being just a product. GORUCK has sought their respective paths for guidance and, true to its unique identity, has already been applauded by S.W.A.T. teams and artists alike.

>> Please give me your thoughts. We're walking into ESPN in a few minutes so I'll largely be out of the loop for a while. Also, we're having a meeting with Will at Tough Mudder tomorrow in Brooklyn at 4pm. They have asked for some of our favorite photos. Are you cool giving them some? I can easily give them all of Mike's. I'm also asking for their video from the camera etc.

>> Are you around tomorrow? I'd like to swing by with some patches and maybe snag the hard drive to go to TM.

>> Thanks, Jdog

May 13 / Bristol, CT / ESPN Headquarters

It's about what you would expect, other than that it's not some sort of hang out spot for the sports world's elite. The talent here stares at running cameras while sitting down telling the tales of every important athlete in the world. To look the part, though, there is a 24/7 gym on site, basketball courts, a mini soccer field to mark their coverage of the World Cup, and pictures of the world's most famous athletes everywhere. Sports paraphernalia everywhere. Obama's NCAA bracket.

The whole place is definitely a shrine to sports cool, but the empty rooms not on the air, the silent lights, the resting cameras and their memories, the people working in the rooms you won't ever see in the background of any of the on-air shows painted a picture of an operation run by people who love sports and who take a lot of pride in getting it right. Heath was angling both sides of what might be Lebron's last game in Cleveland - nobody knew for sure. His day was long enough to have been over at 5pm but the game was still 3 hours from starting and the coverage ended 90 collapsible minutes after the game was over.

The guys work hard and play hard here, some watch sports on their off time and some can't. You can't miss it when you're there.

There is no escape, and when you're there to cut film all day and stay on top of that world, you get really, really good at what you do.

May 14 / Delsea Drive-In Theater, Vineland, NJ

Robin Hood opening night at New Jersey's only drive-in theater, the Delsea Drive-In.

Jack the movie lover tells me as we're rolling in that he's never been to a drive-in before. For me, it takes me back to Ohio as a kid when you paid by the car and had to sneak in cold cuts and pop to keep the costs down or else by the second movie I'd be unruly and complaining about being starving and my dad would tell me sarcastically to whatever I ordered: they don't exactly give 'em away here, do they?

So I learned real quick to feel guilty about overpaying for food, or worse yet having someone else overpay for me, and to be happy with what we had. And tonight we had no food, only some semi-cold beer left over from Connecticut next to the two pups we had to sneak in.

The car was humid like the night, the dogs were panting the whole time which made it hard to hear the movie. But we made do with what we had and, you know, it was even better than I remembered.

May 15 / Wilmington, Delaware

David Bromberg Big Noise in the Neighborhood Concert

==Java ate leftover organic prime rib with a hippie in the parking garage en route to being shut out from the concert.== He was pissed. Jack took the dogs out, then sprinted to the shitter, must have been something he ate. I left too. The vantage point from the perimeter was even more poetic. Lots of dogs there, some with their owners, some sleeping, some wishing they could play frisbee inside the fence.

All happy to be there on the lawn, taking it in with mothers and fathers, hippies and bankers, sons and daughters with infants and toddlers. Soccer balls, frisbees, hacky sacks and outdoor beer drinking abound on a lawn taking in a concert on the river. A summer concert on the river.

Finally, a summer concert.

May 15-16 / Baltimore, MD

Casual daytime beers on Nick's pier. Orioles vs. Indians at Camden followed by a block party with live music at Federal Hill. Beers out of someone's cooler, smiles and a sense of community all around, not replicable inside any of the bars right around the corner, so we stayed on the street.

May 16-19 / Washington, DC

Helped move my aunt and uncle out of one house in the suburbs to another in different suburbs. These were wholly unequal experiences, wholly unequal harbingers of emotion, as the first summons and will always summon the memories I love of a girl I lost.

The house where she lived during her first year at the Agency. Where I visited her every weekend I could, where my family took her in and did what they could to make our lives just a little easier. So that she had someone besides nobody to live with while I was at Fort Bragg for training.

The house where she brought Java back to, the weekend before she left for West Africa with him.

Now it's a reminder of the family that I was not meant to have, the happiness that couldn't sustain itself. And so as my aunt and uncle moved, and as I helped them move, I moved, too, further along a path away from where I am no longer.

Away from the good, away from the bad, away from the pain, away from the failure of two young faces to see each other as they are. Away from a place I do not envy as I once did.

But still towards a love that grows, though love grows differently alone with but memories, imagination and time to reflect on who we are and why we love the people that we do.

Though my address has changed, I will always miss and love Emily.

Java's first weekend with us. Our last together before Em left for Abidjan.
DC - 2007

Along the C & O Canal

Between May 16 & 19 / Great Falls, MD

Java's return to Great Falls and the C&O Canal - the last time we were at the lake here, we were on the lake and Java was just a puppy. January 2007. The lake was frozen, a rarity in this part of the county. Java slipped all over the place like a baby giraffe learning to walk.

Now he swims with the best of them, out and back, out and back, always eager for one more as far out as I can throw it. Ashe lingers by the shore mostly, waiting for Java to come back so I can throw it out again until everyone's worn out enough to sleep really well.

May 19 / Richmond, VA

This city always reminds me of the adventures I've already had here. The adventure that follows me with smiles in tow to the places I discovered one surreal day some three lifetimes ago. Emily was in Washington, DC, I was stationed at Fort Bragg, NC. I got out of our small unit tactics phase, which had been 5 weeks long in the woods, on a Saturday, and had to be back at Bragg at 0430 Monday morning.

We met at the Jefferson Hotel downtown and spent Sunday discovering Cary Street, a wholly friendly slice of the urban south, as dog friendly and warm as any part of any town. Sticky Rice, homemade ice cream, and a World of Mirth. No matter the love and love lost, these places always make me think of her. And smile. **Pretending to think I could rediscover places in a familiar town was every bit the failure I expected.**

Time may dampen the association, but Richmond is wholly ours. It felt like a walking tour of memories still fresh, still poignant, great memories that always run astray no matter how hard I try to isolate them. For now they just sit and linger, casually scented with her distinct Burberry perfume. I can't run nor will I always want to. But now is not then and now is all I've got.

May 19 / Richmond, VA / Dog Night

Minor league baseball is a little slice of heaven. Throwback heaven, how I imagine the 50's would have been.

Sometimes I wonder if I would have fit in a little better back then, if the slower pace would have suited me. Or was it that much different at all? Were fathers still stressed about money and marriage, were mothers still the center of a little boy's life? Did people have the same struggles? A little cozier with all the same reasons to come out to the ballpark. Cold beer, friendly fans, the best food - though I had to sift through all sorts of fancy shmancy stuff even in the minors to find the hot dogs and peanuts. Welcoming a new first in a haunted town, Java was my date, as Ashe was Jack's, for dog night to watch the Flying Squirrels play.

The play in the minors is always a little unpredictable, a little worse, and a little more fun, in a laid back and comforting way I can relate to. Whatever is missing from the lack of big leaguers is more than made up for by the effort of singers, dog trainers, circus performers, and, yes, players who have not quite made it.

Frederick

May 20 / Charleston, SC

Ring toss. Burgers. Palmetto. Kayaking to a plantation. Frederick, father of six and son of Charleston, SC, is someone I hope to spend more time with in this lifetime. If only to learn his smile, to find out where it comes from. I met him on the way out of the Blind Tiger - my only favorite hangout in the great southern gem of Charleston - after sharing ring toss, local brews and Frederick's burgers and fries with the table full of southern charm that was sitting next to us on the outdoor patio. Come June 1, Frederick is a really lucky man, as lucky as any, when his family all comes home to Charleston. A family get-together without a wedding to celebrate, without a funeral to mourn. Just to see each other.

==I want to live like this when I get older.== I want my family to not be so fractured, to all be able to live together, or close at least, to never die off but still keep adding more. I hate goodbye's, I hate not seeing my dad enough. I hate not seeing my mom enough. Even as I am the toughest one to pin down, I want the stability of a family that calls one place home, that has infinite roots there, and that gathers there annually. June 1 to pick a date, but any will do. Even if just for one BBQ, one dinner, a few stories around a table with no TV in sight. It may not ever happen - everyone may feel out of place without a 'reason' to get together, without some timely topic to fill the dead air, but such are my dreams and what I pray for with my family whenever I have one someday.

At this stage in my life, the suburbs aren't for me, or I'm just not ready for the suburbs - one of the two - but I always love the time I spend there. Summerville was no exception, hosted by Jack's cousin. Her smile, her laugh, and her aggressive pursuit of a good time with the girls only made sense to me the next morning when her beautiful kids woke up and she was back to answering to 'mom', not just talking about it as a way to share the good, the bad and the ugly with those who could relate - and have been relating to each other for a while now it seems. She was every bit the southern hostess you could ever ask for. Apologetic that her husband was out of town, she led us to the drop spot to kayak along a narrow channel that opens up into the larger intercoastal. I wanted to see a plantation with my own two eyes, for the same reason that I went to the concentration camp at Dacau. The lessons are stronger and more enduring when you feel them where the history happened. We just kayaked over, docked in mid-calf high mud, and I roamed around the ground, chatting up Jo Ann and her beautiful smile, her great laugh for a bit - which made it a real treat to listen to her tell me about the grounds she takes such pride in maintaining for people like me to come and experience.

Jo Ann

May 21 / Savannah, GA

To Vinnie's with the dogs, we took the long way along the boardwalk and through the town with a fair share of my memories. Seeing Wilco at the Trustee's Theater with Emily, I kept that ticket stub in my wallet for years, until just recently, as a reminder of what a good time I had in this town some years ago. February 18, 2005, months after the Bush re-election, Jeff Tweedy was still pissed, talking in the middle of the set about a Veteran he had spoken to on the street before the show started, who confirmed for him that the war was pointless. As I was still in training, probably off to a war deemed 'pointless' by someone who would likely never find any war meaningful or worth sacrificing for himself, I just wanted him to get back to playing music. Eventually, he did, and I went back to being comfortable in the theater again.

That night Emily and I sprinted to Vinnie's after the show to grab a bite. It was one of those lucky deals when we just made it instead of just missed it. And so I found myself back at Vinnie's, this time sitting outside on the public patio with the dogs, Jack and Sara. $3 beers to go and a hell of a large pizza, by the end there was one slice left standing. Vinnie's won, I guess, but the good times were ours. And the guys and gals working there, so nobody lost.

Sneaking the pups into a cheap motel in the burbs, drinking Busch.

Early wake up, breakfast in town at Holiday Inn express, off to home in Jacksonville.

May 21 / Ponte Vedra Beach, FL

Being at home is always the only way to feel truly at home. On the heels of DC, Richmond, and Savannah, the memories of my past life were inescapable and affecting my day to day ability to be in the moment. As I usually do in such cases, I close off my thoughts and keep to myself. Harder in a car, I possess a professional ability to do it nonetheless.

The beach house where Em and I spent last summer, with Java, as we 'tried to work it out' - whatever that meant, driving by the church where we were married, still talking about it because it comes up more at home than elsewhere.

I'm happy to leave home, sad to leave Java behind, but Em needs to see him, too, I just can't imagine never seeing that dog again. He loves me as much as anyone or anything has ever loved me.

Em seems to be sending feelers to me on getting back together. I'm just not in that place anymore.

I did all I could to keep her, to keep her from up and leaving for Brazil, but off she went, my great mistake for what I could not do some years ago and now I have to pay the price in failure.

If humility is a good thing, and I believe that it is, her name for me is Emily, the love of my life who slipped away.

Adding another car to the summer so that Jack can drive around on his own terms and visit stores is liberating to me. It feels like a legitimate business, on our own terms, more and more by the day. As he plots his course, I plot mine.

Unfortunately Java will be missing next month, it's gonna be hard on me, but God doesn't give us anything we can't handle.

So many people have such real problems in life, I'm distraught and misty-eyed thinking about leaving my dog. But I still can't feel all that apologetic about being so sad to leave him, about feeling sorry for myself.

I just really need him around.

So many great memories with Java at the beach

Home cooked meal at my mom's. Is there anything better?

Better than going out, better than the nicest restaurant in town, I love the whole process. The cooking, the talking, the food, the clean-up, the catching up that is so much more personal at home than it can ever be at a restaurant.

No need ever to lean in and whisper, I am who I am and she is who she is, no formalities at all.

This is the quality time, dinner with mom and the dogs, that I really miss in life when I'm away.

When it goes on too long, it always reminds me that one day, as my grandparents have left us, my mom will leave me.

I'll long to make up for my difficult teen years with as much time later in life spent around our dinner table, wishing that everything could have just worked out for her and Mike, but really just glad to spend time with her and love her while I can still visit.

On Sat, May 22, 2010 at 6:04 AM, Emily <█████████████
███> wrote:

> you know, i realize that it's not easy to write back every time, especially when the questions appear to be heartless and devoid of emotion. the truth is, i'm getting cold feet on the making of our separation permanent in a few weeks. strangely enough, as fate would have it, every time i work up the courage to call you to beg for forgiveness, you don't answer your phone. i think we both have looked major turning points in our relationship in the eye and let them slip away unnoticed.

i had a dream about Java last night. i miss him terribly.

> Em

From: Jason McCarthy <███████████████>

Date: Sun, May 23, 2010 at 11:09 AM Subject: Re: To: Emily <
███████████████>

> hey Em, i don't think that there is any part of this that i ever assume is heartless or devoid of emotion, as it certainly is a very emotional time for me made more so by a pending degree of finality. it is the emotional aspect that i am trying to avoid, sometimes with better success than others, but it's really hard for me. and i assume for you, too. and will be for a very long time. please keep me posted on the legal stuff, as i have zero contact with your/our lawyer and beyond reading the legal documents which seem to pretty clearly state that we both have to attend the court date, i have no idea what is going on. as for Java, he will be in jax at my mom's when you get home to florida. i think he'll do better with my mom because case and cassie are home and have promised me they would take him to the beach daily. he has also become quite aggressive about food. very aggressive in fact, you should be really careful feeding him when he's around other dogs when you're back. moving forward with Java, i don't really know how productive a very emotionally charged conversation about Java will be when i'm back in florida july 3-ish. i think that we both have very emotional ties to Java, with very strong cases for why he is our dog and what is better for Java, so at the end of the day you need him and want him, and i need him and want him, so we should probably go to someone and let him or her decide. i think that at the end of the day it will relieve a lot of anger (though maybe not sadness) towards the other (between you and me) based on whatever is decided. i don't really want to be angry with you, but i am not in a place where i can just voluntarily give Java to you without feeling just that, which i don't want. i will spare you the long saga on my emotional attachment, because that's exactly what it is and I'm trying to keep things as unemotional as possible, as i said, sometimes with more success than others. as for your stuff, yeah, it came about last second. i had a renter move in on May 5, the day I left and a week before i was expecting to leave (i took my exams from the road) and life was hectic. I did the best i could and nik and katie were totally fine with keeping your stuff in their basement. xoxojase+jav

PS i already forgive you, Em, and i'll always love you, there's a lot of you in this little heart of mine here.

May 23, Sunday / Mom's birthday

Sunday Church with mom, a special on parenting, which was not really up my alley, but time with mom on her birthday doing what she prayed for was meant to be. Part of the service was Oliver North on screen talking about the bravery of soldiers (during a service?), everyone at church mesmerized by what it is that America's bravest have done and sacrificed.

It makes me really awkward to stand up when asked to do so, to be singled out as having been in the military. And yet I want people to understand more, not just appreciate, what goes on for those who deploy into harm's way.

The cost that it bears.

For me it was a marriage, the life that marriage represented. It doesn't have to be that, but it manifests itself in a million different ways, and those are just the million that I've seen. There are more no doubt. The sacrifices are real and perhaps many of them unnecessary, but they happen.

And at the end of the day, understanding may start with me standing up a little taller and hanging out a little longer after church to share my story, my stories, to try to help people understand their appreciation for which I am and was and will be so grateful.

From: Emily <███████████████████>
Date: Sun, May 23, 2010 at 2:10 PM,
Subject: Re:
To: Jason J. McCarthy <███████████████>

so you want to take me to court over Java? didn't you always admit to people that he was my dog? you don't even want to give me the chance to make the decision about what to do with my dog? i'm not sure i can ever forgive you if you take me to court and take away Java from me.

From: Jason McCarthy <███████████████>
Date: Sun, May 23, 2010 at 3:17 PM
Subject: Re:
To: Emily <███████████████████>

i'm not going to respond to this for a while.

From: Emily <██████████████████>
Date: Sun, May 23, 2010 at 8:21 PM
Subject: Re:
To: Jason J. McCarthy <██████████████████>

please, jase. i'm just upset about you wanting to go to court after we agreed, in a heartfelt exchange, otherwise. i don't want to fight for Java in court. i was hoping we could try to discuss this in person first but apparently you have no faith in either of us doing the right thing. you have no clue what i was prepared to do regarding Java or otherwise, what i was going to ask you for, what i was hoping for us. you don't give me a chance. as for what you can do for me, you can please drop off Java at my mom's house, i would prefer to not have to pick Java up out at the beach right when i come back and i am phone/car-less.

Brown

May 24 / Asheville, NC

Monday, a new week, the morning brought me to tears on the beach with Java at sunup. Leaving that dog behind, even to be with Em, who is the only person I really feel good about leaving him with for any period of time at all, digs up so many memories I'm trying to move beyond.

Love and loss. Separation. The epic struggle to make it all right in the nick of time. And the failure associated with not being able to do that. She will always be my biggest regret, my biggest failure, and the source of humility that comes along with getting it wrong the first time and not having a second chance at love. Or that life.

Asheville by 6pm, rolling straight in to check out Mark's record shop, Harvest Records. Brown grabbed my attention right away, chilling on the stool at the counter, obviously there for the long haul. Sara caught up with Mark while I chatted Brown up. Off to California soon to visit his cousin, planning to stay a week and extending through a month for the good times. **A different version of adventure seeker, he wanted to head West just to 'do shit and have an adventure'.** Music to my ears to see him smile, as if he knew how lucky and ridiculous to outsiders it was to seek out adventure on his own terms.

I just liked his style as he made no real apologies for picking up and leaving, for hating big cities full of people, for leaving Jacksonville FL where he lived for 8 years until 'she' made it too tough there for him, for doing what he wanted to do now, and for doing it with his family in tow.

Camping off the Blue Ridge Parkway is a must. Hotels shmotels, there's nothing like a campfire and sausages, beer, and music. We invited Mark and friends up. Brown didn't seem to fit into that equation. Luckily they didn't show up till about 1130pm, 30 minutes into the fire it took this Green Beret three hours to finally get going. In my defense, not that any of my boys would care for my excuses, we were in the middle of a torrential downpour, it was raining, the wood was wet. Saturated for the first two hours until Sara went and bought some 'dry' wood that wasn't all that dry. I always miss the time around the campfire, the time with friends who can just show up and share a night and be on their way, or stay, it's their choice. But without the Blue Ridge it would have gone differently. Dinner sausages three hours in the waiting wouldn't have tasted near as good, local brews wouldn't have had quite a rain drenched frustration to soothe or my perseverance to fuel. While I don't mind the rain, maybe next time save us a clear sky or two?

I made a U-turn to come back & get this shot. Such a fun drive in the fog.

May 25 / Asheville NC

Early wake-up to the pitter-patter of raindrops on wet ground. Chance of forest fire zero percent even if you were the malicious type.

The crackling of the fire long gone replaced by the clean up of bottles strewn about.

Rain always inspires a hasty departure, packing up the tent as quickly as possible to hit the road to whatever's next.

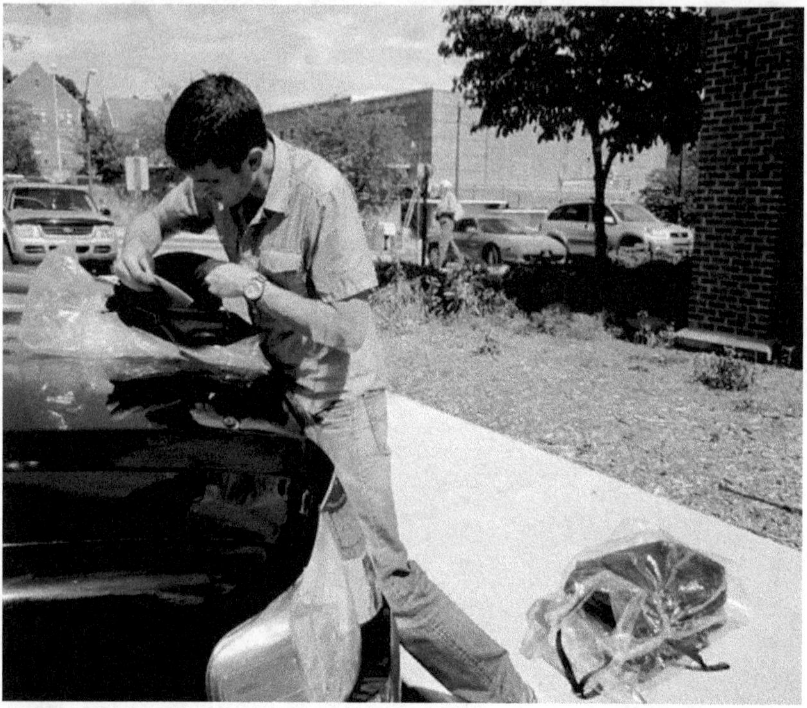

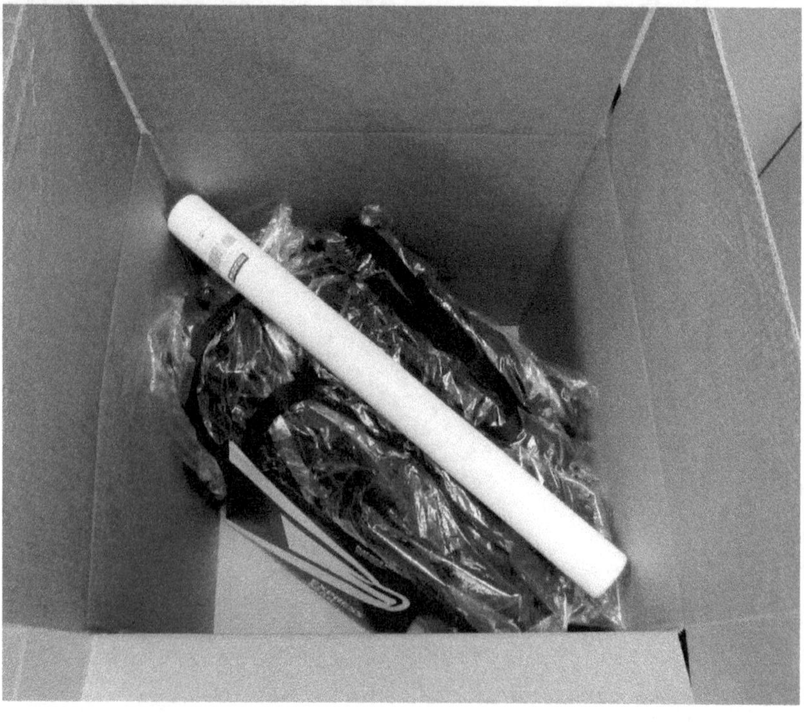

May 25th / Asheville, North Carolina

Detour to the Post Office to get an order out to our first retail shop Sugarcube in Philadelphia.

3 Rucks.

May 25 / AB Emblem / Weaverville, NC

Patches have been one more nightmare to solve for. Ten different places, samples with frayed edges, sharp edges, fraying threads.

We joked it was easier to build the bags than to find a patch manufacturer.

Happened upon AB Emblem referral from a referral from a referral. Seems like they'll be able to do the job. Time will tell.

Also looked at the internal labels for the rucks. Some machine out of England.

Samantha

May 25th / The Wedge in Asheville / Around 4pm.

It came highly recommended. Local recs are always the right answer, off we went. Peanuts and home brew. Always the right answer.

As is the story of Samantha, part-time, best-smiling beer pourer you could hope to get, who works through the arts in Asheville to bring jobs to underprivileged and usually minority families, bridging the gap between this and that side of the tracks. New housing, new chances, new opportunities for people who are really struggling, many of them children, even to eat. It shouldn't exist in America, and I'm ashamed how little of this version of suffering I truly know, but I'm grateful to people like Samantha who are out making a difference, one day, one job, one smile at a time. There's a twinkle in her eye and an extra softness to her smile when she speaks proudly about her work in town. There are so many thankless jobs that go underappreciated, too often we as a society underestimate ourselves, we ask too little of each other only because we forget what we're capable of doing in the name of charity and goodwill, in the name of helping others in our spare time and as a matter of daily life. We forget what our daily lives should look like in favor of what they tell us they have to be.

Beers at Jim's, a fine host with southern roots firmly anchored in the home we casually enjoyed. A day-to-day life so different from mine, so proud to be from the same town where he raised his two girls, where he is happily married to Beth, who has similar roots and a similar sense of proud self-identity in the South. The Asheville South with Asheville roots. Sushi for dinner among old hippies and young hippies. Nobody here has no hippy in them, even the most buttoned-up of them all seem to enjoy sharing the town with everyone except the bounce-backs, the Floridians who got tired of the Jersey shores and bounced back to Asheville and its laid back style and laid back climate instead. Everyone has to have something to bitch about I guess.

Time to go. Tip-toeing around in the morning has distinct sounds when it's in a new place for the first time. The smiling and gregarious become staid in their routines, even the most agile disruptions can seem a major annoyance. Coffee does wonders for the world, especially mine. Jim's home brew was good and stiff, he and Beth gave us all the proper southern courtesies you could ever hope for, but when it's time to go, it's time to go, only with the promise of return trips did it seem right.

Talking your way out of a ticket

- Always refer to the Officer as Officer.

- Admit wrong-doing, tell them some reason why you were speeding. Something human. In my case, it involved GORUCK and trying to finally get home (to Ohio) after forever on the road.

- Ask very nicely if there's any way they can cut you a break.

- You have to do it before they take your license and insurance back to their cruiser.

- At that point, whatever happens was meant to be.

- And thank the Officer - no matter what. It's good karma.

Cliff

May 26 / Beckley, WV

Cliff tells a tale with the best of them. Mostly tales told with smiles on the hardships of daily life, all the while convinced that the purest, most honest day's work is done by miners, in the mines, with fellow miners. That's the value to him, the purity, the honesty. I would have enjoyed working with him for the last 40 years, even at the expense of doing it in the mines of West Virginia, a wholly foreign concept to me. I have infinitely more respect for the dangers our miners face, for the life that they lead after the tales I heard, the work sites I saw, and the pictures of men that spoke to the difficulty of their conditions in a thankless grind of repetition.

There are no dishonest days of work in the mines. I assume the camaraderie is high down there.

==Miners and soldiers share a lot in common.== They do as they're told, there is a lot of grind to deal with, and everyone accepts the risks of the job.

And from time to time there are funerals to attend for men lost too soon.

And it never gets easy.

And sometimes you have to choose the harder path.

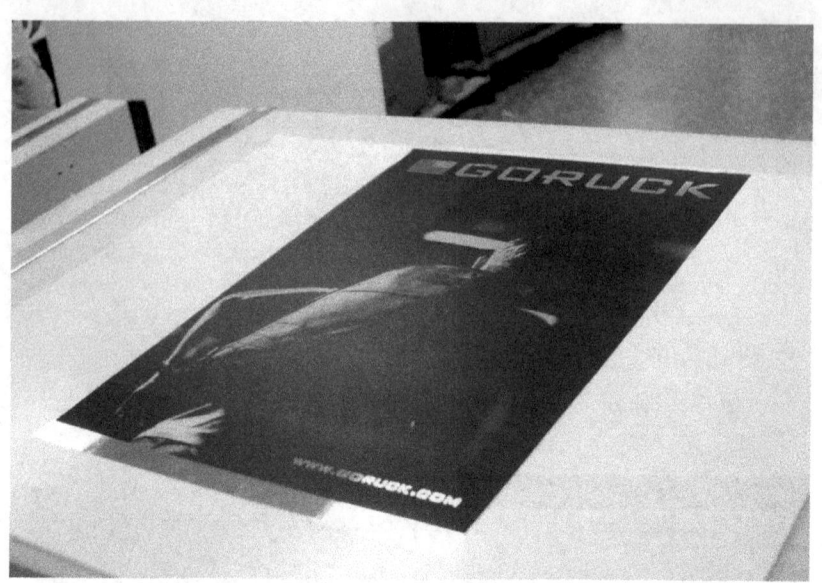

We still have a ton of these left at GORUCK HQ

May 27 / Dayton, OH

[arrived the night of the 26th, late, showed up at dad's work, got the tour of the shop, drank till 230 in the garage]

There are few times so cherished as drinking beer with my father in his garage. It's a wholly sacred place, a testament to all that he's able to do, to make with his hands. To fix cars and build motorcycles. As a kid I thought he could do just about anything in the world in his garage. ==Part of the reason I joined the Army was to live up to my father's standards,== and I did, and I did it well, so while I still can't build a bike or fix a truck, I'm old enough to be jealous of my father without feeling bad about it.

I just enjoy shooting the breeze with him in there now. Till 230, talking about my grandparents' house that's finally on the market, my grandmother's final resting place, what my grandfather would think of my supply chain management.

We chatted about Sturgis, Lake Tahoe - anywhere my dad's ever been that's on our target list. I can only imagine his desire to help me succeed - as he enlists all his buddies at his print shop to do this and that side job for me. And they get it. Knowing the guy that can tell these guys to do things is way less fun than knowing the guy who actually runs the machine, who helps because he wants to. As a kid, I always went to pick my dad up from work in the summers - my grandmother would drive me, casually racing in her convertible Lebaron - I dreaded the smell of the place but loved to see my dad and his buddies. The ink smell was too much for me back then. No ventilation, low ceilings, and presses everywhere. No way it was good for the guys.

The new place, just outside of town, has ceilings like a skyscraper, clean air, less noise. Hell, the place probably cleans itself, with a computer. But the charm is gone. I didn't recognize charm when I was a kid until I got older and saw what charm wasn't. But the guys are all great, the same guys mostly, talking about how long till retirement, how their kids are doing and what they're up to, the promise of fun that summer holds for them and their family, visiting relatives, camping out, boating on the lake. I love these guys, always have. NASCAR, cornhole, Harleys, pick-ups, corn on the cob with lots of butter and real Bud. Always so much to catch up on.

Fred aka Papa

May 27 / Dayton

Montgomery Inn, Reds game.

I love Ohio and couldn't be more proud to call it home. Even though Florida is home now, my roots are Ohio, the Midwest.

Montgomery Inn, the original, takes such pride in Ohio, in the Reds, the Bengals, Ohio State. Memorabilia with an Ohio slant to go with my favorite ribs. It's always a treat. My grandfather took us, it's a place that is just a little too far from Dayton to go often but when you do it's a treat and always worth the time.

Ohio-friendly waitresses, Ohio home brew, Ohio-made BBQ sauce. Wet ribs are the specialty, a full slab of course.

It's almost too much, but there's always room for one more.

Memory lane with Pete Rose, Deion Sanders, Dave Concepcion, and my grandfather. Great American Ballpark is no Riverfront: the place is too posh. Playstation stations - the game used to be the entertainment - but it's the closest thing I have to the baseball games of my youth, so I love it. Every minute of it.

--------- Forwarded message ---------

From: Jason McCarthy < ██████████████ >

Subject: Map plus dates one week out

To: Jack Barley < ██████████████ >

Sara < ██████████ >

AJB / Alex < ██████████████ >

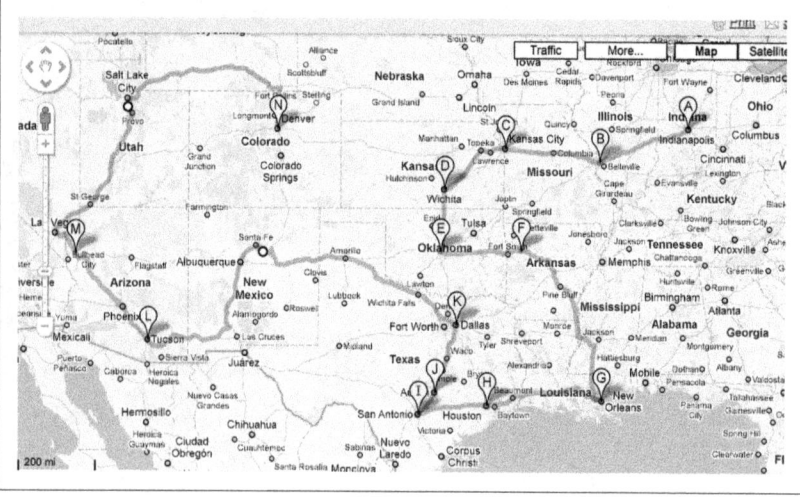

Hey y'all -- Living the dream.

Here are my thoughts on the route, picture attached: Sara, I cut out the Tennessee portion (apologies to your family for the early and inaccurate heads up) because we are back in this area post Daytona Beach July 4 and pre-Dayton Air Show July 16. Memphis is a perfect stopping point at that time. We will go to your friend's house in Jax after the race in Daytona. 30 May: Depart Indy for St Louis 31: St Louis 1: KC 2: Find something in Kansas to do en route to OK. Sleep in OKC (I have family) on 2 June 3: OKC - OKC bombing museum, depart to the Ozarks in AR, 4: Ozarks camp out 5: something en route to New Orleans (it's 550 miles from the Ozarks) 6: New Orleans -- need a place to stay (I have one contact through Emily that would happily take us). 7-8 : Volunteer New Orleans (Sara, please work on this. Jack, you need to be here for this. if Jessie would like to join and stay those dates as well, she should plan on volunteering with us. This is one of our real signature events so we should spread the word to try and get people to join us.) The part below is less thought out because we're waiting on some tips on the Colorado portion of the trip, when we need to arrive there etc. I need to spend some time with the factory there, too, but we're in Colorado until the 27th of June when we start making our way back to Florida -- probably through Chicago. We may stay longer certain places than this or choose to stay longer in Texas where I have some good contacts. 9: Houston 10: San Antonio 11: Austin 12 Dallas New Mexico Arizona Utah Wyoming - south Colorado Pikes Peak climb June 22 - Rockies baseball game in Colorado June 26-27 Fort Collins, CO Brewers festival. July 4: Daytona Beach Florida portion, Key West Alabama Atlanta Tennessee: Memphis, Nashville Oxford, MS Mammoth Cave, KY Corvette factory, KY July 15/16: Dayton, OH Midwest tour prior to Chicago August 1 for the half marathon.

There was a lot of shit
to clean up last year

On May 28, 2010, at 5:33,

Emily <███████@gmail.com> wrote:

> happy birthday, loml. hope this one is better than the last and
> that many more are in store. love Em (dp)

From: Jason J. McCarthy <███████@gmail.com>

Date: Fri, May 28, 2010 at 7:54 AM

Subject: Re: xoxo

To: Emily <███████@gmail.com>

Thanks Em, birthday lover that you are you found me despite the fact that I canceled it from my facebook info ;) Xoxojase

May 28 / Happy Birthday

The Golden Nugget, back from a fire in 2006, is where my grandmother wanted my birthday breakfast, so that's where it was. It's good people serving good food with smiles. There's always a line and the coffee comes before you want more.

I don't know the owners - someone in my family probably does though - but I can imagine there was a time when they thought about shutting the place down after the fire, the work it must have taken to bring it back, to the same quality standards, must have been frustrating. Out with the old while still trying to keep the best that remained of the restaurant where I used to eat weekend breakfasts with my grandfather. It wasn't as nice as the new place, but the charm was always there. The new place gets a pass in my book, though, because they had to rebuild. It was not the new Yankees Stadium, built next to a perfectly good field so that the box holders would have to pay more.

Golden Nugget didn't add Playstation stations or any such frills other than maybe Splenda packets - they kept it about the same, as much as possible. My only regret is I was too full by the end of it for ice cream and pie. Yes, at breakfast.

My grandmother gave me my grandfather's old money clip — I hoped she was right

Open road to Indy to get to the race.

Speed, heat, and an event properly billed as the greatest spectacle in racing. The race is simply a backdrop for the event. I passed up the chance to go as a little kid because I thought it was too hot outside. I've regretted that ever since, even though I probably wouldn't have had nearly as good of a time as I did making this go round my first.

There's a buzz in the air at this event unlike any other I've been to, the infield is incalculably huge - even when I found out there was a golf course on it I couldn't comprehend. Exhausted from taking pictures and racing around all day, we had a minute or two in some A/C before figuring out what to do next. If it wouldn't have been my birthday, I would have driven to a bed and crashed. But there is some internal pressure to maximize the special days that I have in life, and birthdays fit this bill, so Sara and I hit the town.

Rathskellar / Indianapolis, Indiana.

The Slippery Noodle came highly recommended as the oldest bar in town, but a cover charge for a band not playing for two hours was a turn-off, so we wandered around to find Rathskellar, a place straight out of Bavaria with the same flavor of smile I saw at Oktoberfest some years ago. The polka band came out, I didn't even know what a polka band was before we got there. In this case it's a bunch of great guys - a LOT of guys with a LOT of different instruments - that love playing together so they do it when they can, usually 4-5 times a year. Mostly covers, songs everyone loves. Day jobs pay the bills. I had as much fun at this concert as at any I've ever been to. Dancing and singing and laughing, catching the smiles with my eyes and my camera. Chatting with the guys during, and after, mingling among the crowd into the wee hours. Until it turned bad.

Sara came back, after heading unannounced to the car and sending me a text that I should do the same. Well, I was talking to some girls and didn't really want to head back to the car. So I told her I'd see her the next day.

She came back, which took a while since the car was pretty far away, to linger around and said that it wasn't an option her leaving alone. My expectations were that she could figure out how to get to a hotel in the suburbs with a computer, wireless card, and credit card. Her expectations seem to have been that I would take care of all this.

There is baggage this year on my birthday.

Last year Emily and Java missed their flight to come back to the states from abroad, instead they showed up two days later into NYC, where I drove to to pick her up, and there the weirdness began that lasted until she left this past January for Brazil via Florida.

Indy 500

It's not fair to others to bring baggage into situations, but I'm human.

This year, the present. For the life of me, at the time I couldn't understand why I needed to figure out a hotel for Sara, (I still don't), but I said mean and hurtful things about how she needed to be a big girl and figure things out. So she said 'you fucking ruined your own birthday', and that this wasn't working out and that she was going to the airport. "Fine" preceded a silent, long walk to the car.

I started pulling her bags out for her when she said she wasn't going anywhere. Tears. Crying. I told and asked her let's not discuss this right now, but on it went. Sadly.

Mean and terrible things were said on both sides. The second girl I've ever cussed at, and the first took me 5 years to get to that point. Here we were two weeks in with apparently 15 years of friendship working against us. In this case I guess "I fucking ruined my own birthday" - I was dancing with a pretty girl until Sara came back and dragged me outside the bar. Everything went south.

Ultimately we left so I could drive her to a hotel.

There had to be a boundaries talk, a talk about how we're co-workers, which sucks. We're just supposed to be old friends.

I said I was sorry and she just said that she just wasn't there yet. But she also didn't leave for the airport and I wondered why not.

An Iraq War Veteran & ZZ Top

May 29 / Indianapolis, Indiana

Sara disappears all day with the car to the movies or whatever she did, texting later that she needed to get away. I didn't want to deal with the emotions, I'm not suited to dealing with those right now, I'm sorry for this.

My tank is empty after giving all that I had to Emily only to be left amidst pain. And life went on, and it is going on, better by the day, but scars take time, even as hints grow of tearing them anew. It's not fair, no doubt. I have my weaknesses as do we all.

I've been through too much to be normal right now, the epic of love and war and loss and failure, the miserable conditions of training and the life of a soldier. The regret, oh how the regrets kill me when I stop to think.

I worked thanklessly in the motel, not stopping and not thinking.

Dad got to town at 6 or so, a welcome arrival twenty minutes after Sara got back. We all drank a few beers, then my dad and I headed downtown to check out the concert. Awful, cheap, and trite. Mark Wahlberg was the big attraction. Cell phone city. Herding up the beer drinkers is never the right answer. If you're gonna do something, do it right and let the people have fun. Maybe it was great and the problems were mine, though.

Back to sleep at Motel 8.

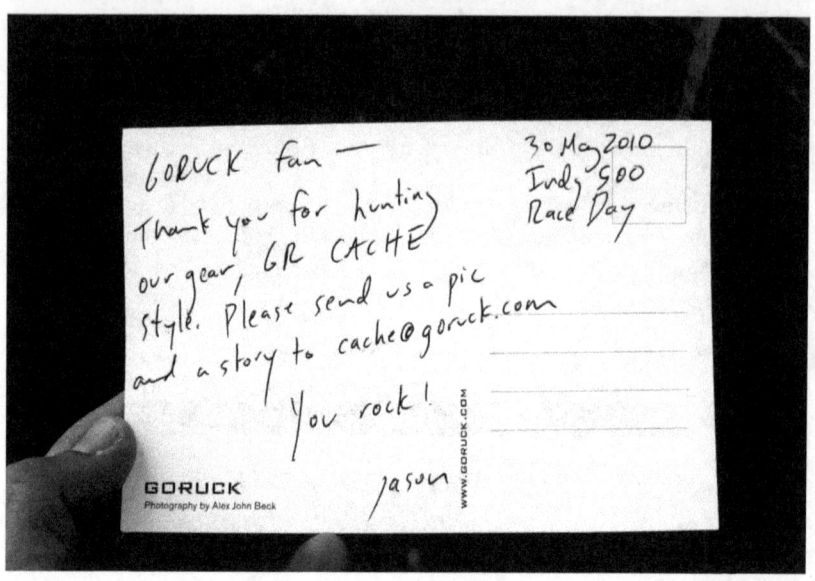

Cache #1 — Indy

May 30 / Indy 500

Wake-up, Starbucks for breakfast, drive to Race. Park in Norman's lot, the $10 lot next to the $20 corner lot that had more cars (why, I know not), chill out, plant GR CACHE hat, head to race, loved it. Way faster, cooler than I thought. I love the atmosphere, the enthusiasm, the people there. 100 or so laps in the stands, then to the infield.

Debauchery. All the same, glad I didn't stay there too long, though it was probably fun, probably would have been fun to spend more time there, the night prior, in the same vein that Mardis Gras is a good time until you realize after it's gone too far that the fun has worn off with cheap booze and no sleep. It was fun to sit by my dad, to listen to him explain it to me, to tell me the stories of camping out for the days prior, drinking all night, and getting no sleep. Not even bad sleep. It was fun to see other fathers with their sons, to see people taking it all in. And loving it. Such a spectacle should be seen. It didn't matter who won.

I said bye to dad by the car, so glad he came to the race with us, I know how proud he is of GORUCK every time he passes out my stickers or talks to his buddies at the shop about it. It's just one more thing to talk about now that we have less to catch up on with my grandparents, both of whom have passed.

Back to Debbie's place, swim in the pool, Japanese for dinner. Settled in, to bed, slightly tired but not able to sleep. As much as I love it, it's not lying to talk about how great this all is, how I love the challenges, the building of something ours, the safeguarding of the brand at all costs. All the difficulties are part of it. But this is no joke and I understand better than ever my grandparents' culture of a drink or two at the end of the day to unwind. And I understand that even that's not enough sometimes, so I sit in strange beds, sometimes nice, sometimes not, and stare at the side walls, which are also sometimes nice and sometimes not, and run the racetrack in my head for as long as it takes.

My dad & I had a blast.

Basic Training Graduation
Fort Benning, GA 2004
Drill told me and Scott
to "SQUAT" right before
this pic was taken

31 May / Memorial Day / St. Louis

Heading to St Louis after hearing some crazy talk from Debbie, who we were staying with, about how she may want 1,000 GR2's by January for some NFL give-away.

They're probably enough up there in the world that it's not BS, but I'll believe it when I see it.

1,000 bags is a ton of bags.

I was hoping to see my old Drill Sergeant. Last time I saw him I was driving across the country to get from Fort Carson to my new, married life in Abidjan.

Drill was completely out of his element working as a handyman around his neck of the woods, so it didn't surprise me one bit to find out he was contracting in Iraq. Selfishly sad but glad to know that he was happier doing his part with the belief he was making a difference. I had hoped to trade him for one of his hand-carved pipes. Next time.

Reds vs Cards in St Louis. Pujols hit 3 homers vs the Cubs yesterday, hopefully he got them all out of the way for my Reds. Pouring when we showed up so we parked right outside the stadium and sat there for a second, getting ready. I'm still going to go in. It's pouring, everyone is right outside the gates, no ticket taker present, so I just meander on in and have a walk around. Really, really fancy stadium. So red, everywhere, not even a tinge of visitors dissent with the Reds in town. But there was a tinge of the Reds increasing their lead on 1st place. Until they blew it and I left early for a local beer only to have to tell the locals that the Cards looked good en route to two more beers and bed.

Spartacus

June 1 / Kansas City

We had some time to kill, so we went to the Truman Museum. Who knew it was right in Kansas City. The truth is all I want for history seemed about right, how do we get that? Her truth or mine, what about the middle, the compromise. Who are we supposed to blame when the truth doesn't matter. I really have no idea, and wish it were so simple.

BBQ is easier, and Benny's BBQ was our introduction. It didn't live up to expectations for the city at large, but we needed a quick fix of local en route to the Royals game.

Lucky for us, Spartacus and his friends were hanging out in the parking lot next to the stadium. I asked them where I should buy the cheapest tickets, one thing led to another and after shotgunning a beer I was the honorary Godfather of the group, solidified with the summer tale of adventure. Spartacus asked me all about it until his friends brought up his newfound love for eating competitions, which he was eager to talk about. He wanted to travel around next year to all the coolest eating competitions in the country. Not so much the speed ones, but the endurance ones. He had his sights on the 7-pound burger local, that he planned to name. As the first one in the state to do it, it would probably make national news. Or at least state-wide.

I wish it were easier in my daily life, when I have a routine, to just meet people and have a chat about their lives. To get brought into the group with a couple beers, some insight into how people live their lives, what makes them happy. ==The answer is almost always other people. Life is meant to be shared.==

Standing around 50 empty beer cans with a car stereo blasting, the soundtrack to stadium lights. That's really living.

We were still out there well into the 4th inning, eventually deciding to go in and watch a losing cause that everyone loved. Royals Stadium has no bars, nothing fun right around it, but it has one of the best atmospheres around. It was 25th anniversary t-shirt night - the last World Series they won. George Brett is a real local hero. The people smile about their team's lack of success, but they love coming to the park, cheering on their team. Sara and I stayed till the very end and beyond, checking out the waterfalls, fireworks, and sounds of a Kansas City that showed us a great time - so great I didn't want it to end.

June 2 / Kansas City / Oklahoma Joe's

Straight from the airport with Alex to Oklahoma Joe's. I was really, really excited to try the Smokie Joe, recommended by so many all over town - in Kansas City with Kansas City BBQ lovin' put into it. Please do it justice, I thought. One bite and I was hooked. Two and I couldn't believe it was this good. Everything. An American icon. A restaurant nestled in a gas station, like it always was, with huge lines always worth the wait and owners who pass along their pride and love for what they do. I'll be back any time I'm anywhere close.

Wichita, Kansas / outskirts, close enough to see fireworks from the roof

Doug & Teresa

June 2 / Clearwater, Kansas / Klausmeyer Dairy

Doug is the best among us. His first airplane flight was two years ago, to go to an agricultural meeting in Georgia. A little different there, he said, but nice. It's always a smile with him. It's a hard life and one that makes me as jealous as I am of the soldiers I served with who figured out how to have a family life on top of making a difference.

Starry nights in the summertime from the roof, as a family, waiting for the fireworks from Wichita to start. Doug's daughter, Teresa, gave us her first tour of the farm. She sorta hoped for more vacations away from home but she so precociously admired her father it was inspiring to listen to her talk about him.

Last year at business school, I wrote a paper on the Trans-Pacific Partnership and why Obama should not prioritize the concerns over dairy prices plummeting. Doug smiles to keep from giving the impression of complaining when he talks about how dairy prices have plummeted recently and how hard it's been. And yet he got into pumpkins, he got into educating local school children about how a dairy works, how milk magically gets into the cartons at the grocery store. He does it to make ends meet for himself and his family.

I gave him a bottle and he filled it up fresh for me - but only after trying to warn me against trying raw milk for the first time there, saying it has natural bacteria in it that isn't bad, it's just not what everyone is used to anymore. This was my only beef with him, so I cut him off, telling him with a big grin that he could give me all the warnings he wanted but that I wasn't leaving without trying his milk. And there was magic in there, though a different kind from when I was a kid and didn't know how the milk made it to the cartons. The magic lies all around the Klausmeyer farm because of what goes into it. From the people who do it. I wish I had a million dollars to give him. But for the milk and eggs all he asked for was a little bit of money for Teresa for the tour.

He said $40 was way too much, so I gave her $40.

THE SPIRIT OF THIS CITY AND THIS NATION WILL NOT BE DEFEATED; OUR DEEPLY ROOTED FAITH SUSTAINS US

June 3 / Oklahoma City

Oklahoma City National Memorial

Alex didn't get why we would visit this place as part of the summer. I simply tried to explain that this was an important place that everyone should see for what it represents. Myself not knowing exactly what that was, I knew it would NOT be a shrine to our collective anger and scorn directed at the attackers. I knew they would do it right, and I needed to see it.

I needed to see it for myself, so I walked around alone; the gravity hit me from the first second I saw the wall. 9:01 9:03 In the middle is now a reflective pond and chairs to symbolize those who passed April 19, 1995. I remember the huge hole in the middle of the building on TV. I remember the announcers revisiting Waco and that awful mugshot of the attacker. And something about how he was in the Army, a sad fact that makes me madder and sadder now.

I talked to Matt for a long while, a National Park Service ranger on his first temporary posting. He spoke of the honor it was to help preserve the memories of those who passed, of doing them justice for the city, their families, and our nation. He spoke with a passion that transcended his words, a pride to be there that bonded us, as I stood there proud as I could be - not having been there at the time - at the sanctity that this memorial captured.

The hardest thing he ever had to do, in his life, happened when he was on shift on the grounds. A lady came up with a teenager, 17 years old, and asked to walk over to her sister's chair. Matt said of course and was close enough to hear the sister tell her nephew that she knew he hadn't been here yet, but that the chair in front of him was his mother's.

I teared up just thinking about Matt overhearing it, about a 2 year old who never knew his mother, or even her chair, which lights up every night, until now. About it all, the string of events that brought it to the bombing, the pain and suffering that ensued and still ensues. The loss, the people I miss, the innocence of being able to not understand just how awful this was. And is.

But there was a tree.

The tree, which should have suffocated but didn't, which is now stronger than ever from its perch above yet on top of the tragedy. That's what the people remember, this is where I smiled, this part of the grounds is where somehow there was some sense of sense. And so that's what I clung to, and the fondest memories of this place are all here, at the tree.

"our deeply rooted
faith sustains us"

The locals, my cousins, sorta wish that the Memorial wasn't the only thing in town everybody sees. I do, too. OKC is up-and-coming in their eyes, growing strong from people who love it there, where there's more to do than they are comfortable talking about because flying kites next to manmade lakes and minor league baseball games don't immediately mean big time.

But if this is small time, and everyone lives like my cousin Lee, happy to be alive with friends who would do anything for each other, then give us all the small time for the rest of our lives.

With a reminder in the center of town of just how precious every day is.

USPTO PHOTOS - Trademark application
From: Jason McCarthy <█████████@gmail.com>
Date: Thu, Jun 3, 2010 at 1:19 AM
Subject: 77413103 To: <█████████@uspto.gov>
Ms █████,

Thank you for taking the time to review my application for GORUCK.

Could you please indicate if you are looking for pictures like the attached that show the mark GORUCK in use on the products for sale in Class 18 and Class 25?

This was the case at the time of filing for the Statement of Use.

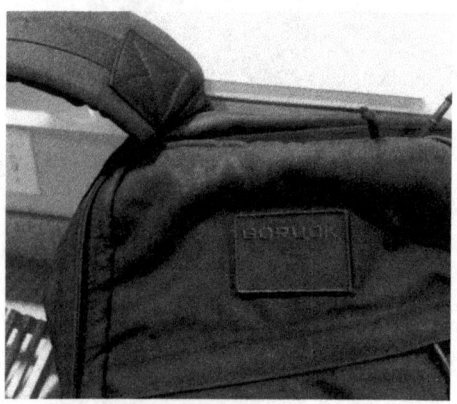

>> > On Thu, Jun 3, 2010 at 1:34 AM, Jason McCarthy
>> > <███████████@gmail.com> wrote:
>> >> hey Em, think i missed a call or two. been a hectic day of driving, just getting to bed in oklahoma city.
>> >> please snuggle with the monster right now for me.
>> >> xoxojase

>> On Thu, Jun 3, 2010 at 10:05 AM, Emily <███████████@gmail.com> wrote:
>> > was it more like you screened a call or four? please let me know when you will be able to accept my call. Java is good, be safe driving. xoxo

> On Fri, Jun 4, 2010 at 2:03 PM, Jason McCarthy <███████████@gmail.com> wrote:
>> it's hard in the car, Em, with Alex and Sara -- didn't seem like the
>> best time to talk to you for the first time since you left for brazil.
>> world cup advertisements and the keane song that reminded me of our trip down there reminded me to write you.
>> i'll try to give you a call when we get to the ozarks tonight. if i
>> have cell phone coverage at all.
>> if not, i'll call you from dallas tomorrow night. presumably your
>> mom's cell is best.
>>
>>
>> i hope you're having a nice time at home with your fam. and Java
>> of course. careful if you take him to the beach. even in PV i got a
>> ticket for not having him on a leash.
>>
>> xojase

June 4 / The Ozarks, Arkansas

My only experience in Arkansas as a kid was driving through it. Interstates rarely give a favorable glimpse, this was especially true in Arkansas' case. The Ozarks have been on the list to visit from the time the list began for this summer. It is indeed a gem hidden from too much of the country, natural beauty with easy access for hikes and swims and rafting.

We found a campsite not far from Cass, next to an inlet to the river. Summers of my youth with my father were often spent on such campsites - in the Midwest, the smells of the river are the same. I might as well be 12 again, too scared to talk to the 14 year old from New York state in the camper next to ours. But here I swim around, at peace because the triggers in my mind take me to a peaceful place. The older I get, the more triggers I have. By the time I'm a grandfather I'll be as reminiscent as mine are, and were, where everything that happens in life triggers memories of old memories. I revel in it, underwater in the creek, backstroke a while, shut my eyes and turn off the now. Off. For just a few priceless minutes, in a creek in Arkansas, I was a kid again and always.

We gathered some wood, I scolded myself for forgetting my axe at the beginning of all this, and I hunkered down to get a fire going so we could grill our brats.

Camping is hard on our bodies, we don't sleep very well, and it slows us way down, but it's necessary to just get out of the grind. It's worth the slower pace, the campfire smells of a time without iphones and blackberries. Those times are gone but the reminders, the places to remind us, still exist and are thriving.

Sitting around the campfire while Sara and Alex filmed the night sky by the river, I again lost myself in thought of the fires my dad used to build for us, the fires I built in the Army - after a night long land navigation movement or in Iraq just to do something different and change up the pace, to get together. The fire calms me in a similar way to the ocean in Florida. In a way that the daily business, the daily day-to-day of life cannot. Because I won't let it - I wish I were simpler about things sometimes. All the more important to seek out a place like the Ozarks.

Swim in its rivers, talk to old friends and new around a campfire, and try to forget the rest of the world.

Hippies dancing with light sticks, Joe with survivor stories, operation after operation, Wakarusa Music Festival that we could not hear one note of despite being pretty close - local wine, PBR boxes, Cassie our new friend from Fort Smith - 20 year old mother on a night out, can't find her friends, partied with us instead.

Joe's Scars

On Fri, Jun 4, 2010 at 1:32 PM, Emily <██████████@gmail.com> wrote:

> i understand, now. just a little sensitive, please forgive me. i can't
> know though if you don't tell me. and not sure what to read into the fact that you need to be reminded to write me, wow. not sure who Sara is but hope all is well with the gang. i do want to talk to you, preferably in person however, i'm doubting you are going to be available before mid-june?

> Java is a sweetie, he's sleeping right now. we have to go pick strike up at the vet now, he was sedated for a bad hot spot. :(Java dropped him off to provide moral support. was wondering when he had heartworm last...

> call when you can, mom's cell is the way to go. xoxo Em

From: Jason McCarthy <█████████@gmail.com>
Date: Fri, Jun 4, 2010 at 2:49 PM Subject:
Re: welcome home
To: Emily <█████████@gmail.com>

i didn't have to be reminded, Em. i think about you all the time.

wounds heal their own way sometime, though.

i just had to be prodded to actually write instead of think.

i almost told you in the last email that Java was due for a heartworm on the 10th. poor strike, he's following george's lead for making himself miserable.

i'm not around that part of the country till right before the Firecracker 400, which is July 4th in Daytona.

I'm glad I left Java there for you or it would have been really hard for you to meet up with us and pick him up; we're not making it farther east
than the Ozarks until we head from Chicago late June for Daytona.

xojase

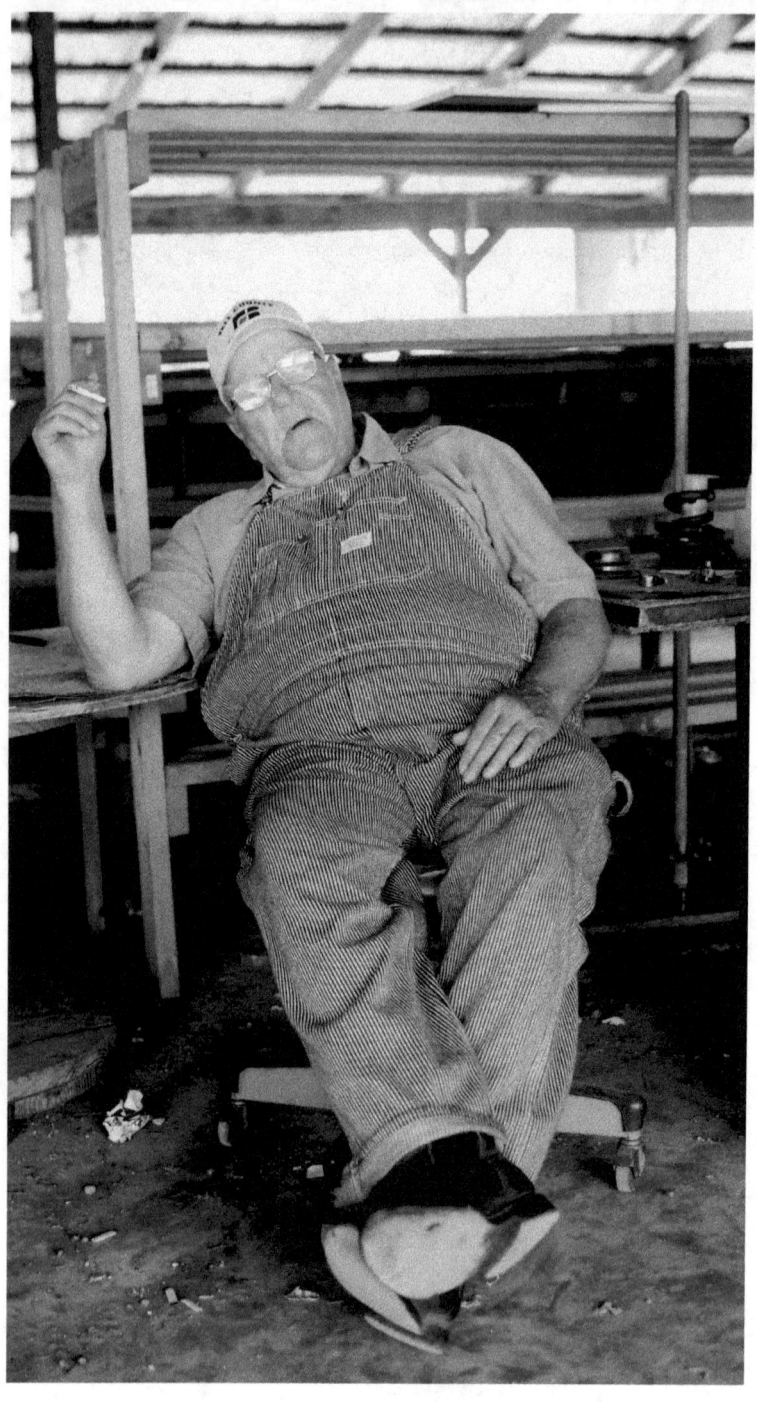

Dale

June 5 / Arkansas

Camping wake-ups, even under Ozark skies, are never as beautiful as the time spent the night before. Rustic nostalgia meets a stiff ground and the stiff ground holds steady.

But the smell of the campfire still lingers, the creek still flows gently.

Ten minutes in the water - just ten minutes - a brief nod to Alex, acknowledgement of how lucky we are to be right here, right now, and we're almost fresh for the long trek to Dallas through Dale's peach farm in Russellville and then Little Rock.

We showed up too late for the peaches. They all left for Little Rock this morning - and while his wife found a couple for us, they wouldn't be ripe enough for 3 or 4 days. Peaches have to breathe as they ripen, so we'll put it in a paper bag. **If it were apples, a plastic bag would be just fine.**

Dale turns 76 next month, and shows the signs of a life spent on his farm. He's ready to retire, life has made him cynical to the conglomerates, politicians, and strangers. We had a nice chat - he cut to the chase on everything going on in his world, the garage that needed organized, the peaches he sent off this morning, his desire to be done with farming. His family doesn't want to take it over and he's 15 years late retiring.

I wish he weren't right. I wish the little guys of the world would stay around en masse. But I know, as he does, that he's right.

The Rodeo in Destin, Texas

June 5, 2010 / Arriving in Dallas

My ma'ams and my sirs return to me real quick when I'm in Texas. At restaurants, at gas stations, with strangers and with the oldest family friends we have. Even family friends always on a first name basis - it's out of respect. It's just how you do it in Texas. And it comes with smiles and big, firm handshakes.

Good to be back in Big-D. Monster steaks on the grill right when we show up past dinner time on Saturday, Bud Light in the cooler - "they're cold and they're free" John says in his big Texas way. He opens one for me and wraps it in a napkin. So we catch up as fast as possible for old friends 20 years separated. Eating Karen's oatmeal chocolate chip cookies for dessert takes me back to when I'd head over to get 'em hot 20 years ago, it also takes me to the care package she sent to me and the guys when we were in Iraq. Every morsel is something special when it's good and sentimental. Always worth catching up with.

June 6, 2010 Sunday / Dallas

Woke up to hot coffee, biscuits, honey, and fruit salad. This was the daily routine for us as guests. Karen had been up since 5, just to get some time to herself. We were looking forward to hitting the rodeo with John. I remember how he used to lasso me when I was crossing his lawn to shoot baskets on his court. Always with a big smile, he'd say 'gotcha!'. Harris is still doing the lasso thing. He trekked out to Destin with his horses, and we showed up for the show.

Good people, Texas friendly all around. Some with their family, some without. John was bummed to miss church, team roping is not usually on Sunday.

It's not the big time, there were no TV cameras, no long lenses, just family guys and gals having a good old time with their horses and their friends. In a hanger full of big-ass fans outside Fort Worth. All in all, the calves did alright in the end, nothing but a lasso here and there, no big deal unless you're the one trying to do it.

Dinner with Bill Stockum at some Mexican joint in downtown Dallas, the only food I want to eat out in Dallas. I'm getting kinda sick of talking about GORUCK all the time, from the get-go, listening to everyone's ideas about strip malls and SEO and what I need to do, but I am a data miner of good ideas, the price I pay. I also like Bill a lot, so it was good fun to chat about GORUCK and the Mavs, an old fave of mine.

June 7 / Monday / Dallas / White Rock Lake

The Rock. I have such fond memories of my mom running the marathon there, of training when we lived in Dallas. Long ago when I thought I would never run because I hated it. The 9 miles or whatever - it was a bit long for me right now, but I had to do it. For the first time. The lake is big, scenic, altogether relaxing. Even though I wasn't ready for 9, it was too nice of a day to not love it, the people so friendly and usually greeted us with a "mornin'" as we crossed paths. **Americans are too friendly, eh? Well I love it, I think it's great.**

Monday night, after computer and website stuff all day + rejecting a bunch of new bags, we head to the Rangers game with the Harrises. Baseball is always a good time, John was so proud of Rangers Stadium, declaring emphatically that it's the best around. It is nice. It's a destination stadium, built where land was cheap and they could set up a city around it (not in Dallas city limits). But it was a blast. Beers, hot dogs, peanuts, and Karen's $12 margarita meant to hold the place of the white wine they didn't have. The Rangers put up a good fight at the end but lost to the Mariners 4-2. They never won enough when I was a kid rooting for them, either. But I kept rooting anyway.

Dallas last night, hung with Harris fam. Steaks on the grill, beers. They're cold and they're free, Harris says again. I say their last names, Mr and Mrs Harris all the time, but don't think most people are comfortable with that anymore. John and Karen, though, and they go by John and Karen to me, still appreciate a ma'am and a sir now and again. Mom has stayed in close touch with Karen over the years, but they didn't have to open their home and hearts to me for 3 days. Texas hospitality is something.

Sara forgot to make her bed after the first morning, came back mid-afternoon to find it tightly pressed. I bounced a quarter off of it it was so tight. Homemade oatmeal chocolate cookies - from my youth at the Harris's house 20 years ago, as well as in 2007 in Iraq - the same recipe, the same happiness. I kept telling her all weekend she must put crack cocaine in them. They're that awesome.

Karen & John

June 8 / Dallas

Said bye to John this morning, Karen once we were off around 1pm. She sent us off with a bath of butterscotch chocolate chip cookies, a wholly new favorite of mine now. Get into these, too.

I miss them already, I need more of the Harrises in my life. So I gave Karen a big hug and told her I'd see her and the boys soon. Hopefully it won't be another 15-20 years.

To Austin. Headed for Lance's bike shop.

Rolled in, straight to Mellow Johnny's. Love that store, way more than a bike shop, it's an icon. Chatted up Chris on the sales floor for a long while, then started talking about GORUCK. He loved the stuff, set up a meeting with their buyer Katie for me for the next day. Wanted to buy a hat off me on the spot. Typically loved single slings, but said he loved our stuff, clear quality.

Back to Ben's place in Austin, John Franklin's friend. Total dump, Sara complained about it of course, even as she got the only free bedroom. Whatever, it's about time for a chat with her. Again. I wonder about some facets of a patience I've tried to develop over the years. The hominess of a friend's friend was never felt so strong with Ben. We barely saw him, and actually spent more time with his roommates, both from Alabama. Ben is too, but the northern part. And totally different they say.

Taco shack the first night en route to TC's Lounge on a recommendation. East Austin, a little less banal than 6th street West Austin. But TC's was way east and regularly housed, by reputation, the best blues in town with an atmosphere of sweat dripping from everything. Where you're encouraged to leave mementos on the walls, which we forgot this night.

So we showed up, not a car to be found. Only TC and a buddy, plus Sugar Baby chilling behind the bar. We ordered some PBR tall boys and joked a bit with TC after walking around a bit, the promise of a packed house never more present than when it was totally empty. Floor fans ready, sweat almost dried, floors broken in by years of dancing, a step-up stage nestled nicely into a corner with tattered posters. Speaker stacks. TC got a little curious with our picture-taking, the walk-around, what we were doing, the mark of a man protecting his brand, and it is a gem, and defending himself against getting ripped off. I'm sure somewhere along the way he's had some deals and some publicity go bad. He was a good ways into his bottle of liquor when he got a little testy on our motives, and much to my dismay I couldn't convince him our motives were purely positive.

TC's Lounge

The night fizzled out and we went on our way, promising to come back the next night just to check out the show and bring a poster or two for them. We went to another outdoor patio that sold beer, on a perfect night, lost in our own little world of adventure. Our guide drank heavily to keep himself entertained on more than our obscure tellings of tales, though this may have been his style anyway.

To bed on couches, already tomorrow. Comfortable couches.

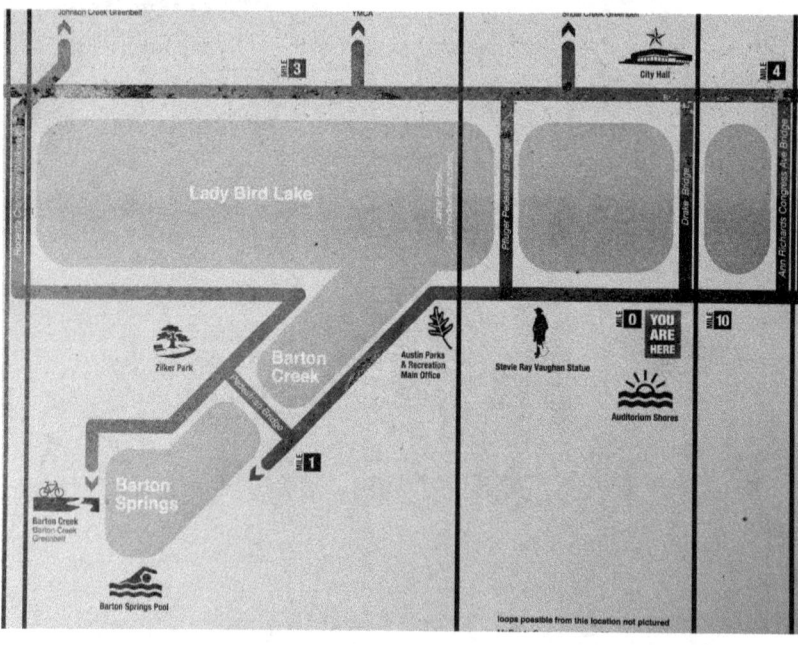

June 9 / Austin, TX / Wednesday

Running by the river downtown in the rain. People don't move to Austin for the rain, but I loved it. One of the few times when I don't have to worry about anything getting wet, running with nothing in my pockets or on my back, the sense of abandon feels good. I'm worn out after 8 miles or so.

The last time I was in Austin was to hire a freelance designer to do the bags; we had a good time and sketched out some cool stuff in the lobby of some big hotel. It didn't work out eventually because I didn't know he couldn't actually build the bags himself. I had hoped he could be our permanent designer, which I thought meant R&D. Live and learn I guess. It all took me so much longer than I had hoped for because I desperately wanted to get it going, fast, faster than it was ready to at that time.

I went for a similar run back then in the middle of the Texas heat - I can't say I minded it back then, in 2008. But today the rain took care of the things racing around in my head, as best as they could for as long as they could.

//

In Dallas last Monday afternoon, waiting for more boxes of bags to show up from FedEx.

Emily called from her mom's house, (904 -███ - ████) a number that always made me smile when I saw it pop up on my phone.

It was the first time we had talked since she left for Brazil last year. It was weird until it wasn't, and weird only when we talked about the past. The present was never that weird at all. Java was front and center. To hear her voice always humanizes the thoughts I have about a fairness between us. I hate to hear her sadness, her pain, that she doesn't have it figured out, that it hasn't worked out. I hate it. And yet I'm distant, I feel her feelers and I still hate feelers. Why can't you just say exactly what you mean. I hate the blame, even when emotion dictates. Especially when emotion dictates.

But it was great to hear her voice, to hear her say she misses me so much, that she loves me. It felt good to tell her that I love her, too. To say what I've tried so hard not to think.

We could fall back into the same trap, or routine - only hindsight and its users could judge. Could we make it work this time? This and so much more was hanging in the air.

She said her town in Brazil was kinda like the Jacksonville of Brazil - I laughed so hard as I asked her how many times she had used that analogy. It broke up something we were talking about that was much tougher. I couldn't talk for a while when she started talking about taking Java back

to Brazil with her, it's just impossible to think about, the build up to those thoughts is so terrible, and yet I feel I could endure it. Over a dog, I know. She said she's asked him if he wants to go to Brazil and he's not sure yet.

It made me really sad but I didn't know how to share that with her. And she had to leave and I had to leave, it was probably for the best so I could start going through bags the FedEx guy brought while we were on our call. I was certain most would fail, which made it even harder to think about our different lives made harder by the promise that was.

How did we get to this point where we're calling each other and saying we love each other but we're not together and she's living in Brazil but back at her mom's house by herself and I'm here, running zippers up and down these rucks, again and again, pulling on shoulder straps so hard I hope they fall out. It'll feel good to break them.

How did we get to this point where she has to ask Java if he wants to go to Brazil and never see me ever again. Still, I wiped my tears, resigned to thinking about her often, happy for her to be back with Java and upset by the cruelty of life, hoping that she hoped to hear from me again, sometime soon.

//

8 miles in the rain over two bridges along a river in Austin, it did me good. Lone Star when done.

Never fully prepared for the day in front of us, life has risk and it's always worth the promise of the next smile from a stranger, phone call from a friend. The steady love of those closest to me.

And so back to life in Austin. I needed some space, happily spent at Jo's Coffee Shop downtown, well within striking distance of my meeting at Mellow Johnny's, which was scheduled for 2pm. I walked in a minute or two early and asked the guy at the sales desk if Katie was in. He asked me all about the rucks, so I gave him the tour of the bags to much agreement and respect (my perspective) - just as Katie came up I was zipping up my GR2 - I asked where she wanted me to show her the stuff, here, there or wherever? And she said that the conference room was full so I went right into it with a big smile.

And she loved it — the concept, the grassroots push, how I said we're trying to build an iconic brand and not just sell things, it has to mean something more. She loved the marketing potential with Wounded Warrior Project in January for their race, and wanted to sell our hats there.

Ben at Hey Cupcake

So those will be on their way first, for our national debut, in Lance's bike shop, with Lance's Mellow Johnny's logo on them. Though I loved the process, sales is not the end all be all. I love the people I talk to, the story I tell effortlessly (at this point) - I don't like to think of myself as just a salesman. Willy Loman with his briefcase. Even though I can smile my way through it.

//

Hey Cupcake, south of town after Home Slice Pizza on the steps in front of a gorgeous night in Austin. A buzz, nice weather, the vibe of outdoor venues. We headed south to see Ben at his stand, full of smiles, eager to talk about what makes the business great. The quality, the relationship with customers, the whole experience. Wes, the owner, wants to sell for life.

Back to TC's, the lot not nearly as packed as I was expecting, the promise of the place so much greater than the Wednesday night reality. Mondays are the night I guess, but I still had such high hopes. Sugar Baby greeted us right away as I gave her the posters and stickers, asked me if I wanted to take pictures, tonight the band wanted me to. TC was chilling in his corner, presumably as always. Until Sugar Baby started choking out a girl who was sitting on one of the tables, drunk. 'This ain't no strip club' led to a little catfight. TC out of his chair, telling the girls 'never, ever come back.' NEVER COME BACK. I love a little catfight. Consequences are so small and the entertainment so high.

We were back to the band. They had a great style and a record coming out soon. Rightfully so. I'd buy it, not just for sentimental reasons. We soaked it up, peacefully, not taking any pictures since TC seemed fired up tonight, and despite Sugar Baby's whispers. Just soaked it in. Sweat drying on the hardwood floor, the speakers blasting, a mellow crowd. And then home to sleep it off before a 9 hour drive to Beck Boots in Amarillo.

Alex wanted to get out of the truck so he could take some pictures of the clouds.

Beck Boots

June 10 / Amarillo, TX / Beck Boots

Gas station en route, Alex asked for a bagel with cream cheese after looking at the menu, the guy laughed at him and said he had never served a bagel and didn't know if they had any. So Alex went to look for something already made, slightly off kilter, and knocked over a bag of chips, then disappeared a ways away while we laughed at his expense. He settled on a breakfast sandwich warmed under a heat lamp.

Coffee to-go on the road through West Texas.

Beautiful driving, winding roads, and greener than the desert you'd expect, not a cactus to be seen.

Pulled into Beck Boots. They were ready for us, like a train ready to depart. Mr Beck greeted us warmly, as fine a gentleman as you would ever hope to meet, knowing only that his assistant had checked out our blog and thought highly enough of us to tell the boss he could meet with us. He was eager to talk about making boots, which he's done his entire life. He was the type of timeless guy who worked hard and made an honest living his entire life, who does it now because he enjoys it, and who is always curious as to what's going on with the generations that will follow him. I respect the hell out of what he's done with the family boots.

He opened up with us about his family, those who have gone before him, and the family that is still around, his eight kids - one of whom who was lost, and one who was meant to take over the reigns. He was amazingly process-oriented, able to think big picture for the next generation of sales coming from pre-stocked boots and Internet sales, from google search engine optimization, and yet the craftsmanship was a caliber not surpassed anywhere.

He was humble about having his name on the boots. Makes no difference he said.

Beck Boots is an inspiration of mine. Stay small and true to your roots, make a better product, in the USA. Charge more, make 6 pairs a day. I count my lucky stars we were able to meet with them. Jeremy (Mr Beck's assistant) is the nicest guy, full of exactly what it will take to move the shop to the next generation of customers. It's about the customers, it's about the heart of the creator.

Say Cheese

June 10 / Amarillo, TX

Coyote Bluff Café. It came recommended by Jeremy at Beck Boots. It was half an hour out of the way to drive west, so I was reticent, but Alex and Sara talked me into it. It was raining and there was a line, at 6pm on a Wednesday?? So it must be good.

Burger from Hell came recommended as the house specialty. I was hungry at the time and these things are so hard to say for sure, but it was at a minimum one of the best burgers I've ever had. Colors on the walls, colors from the lights hung up, colors from the people who work there, and colors from the people who eat there. Everyone loves it. And everyone who's ever been to Amarillo knows about it. And loves it.

There's a lot of brown eating this trip, hamburgers in the summertime one of the staples.

But...the colors were perfect on this one.

Stopped in The Drive in Logan, NM, stayed the night.

I was up till 230 am in the bathroom working. Sara passed out when we got in, Alex up a while later working. Sort of wired, crawled into my bed on the floor, woke up to go for a run, out and back.

Taos, NM / June 11 / Friday

Fixed a flat tire en route. A beautiful drive through Angel Fire and the Santa Fe National Forest. Huge rock had us on the side of the road for the better part of an hour. It could not have come at a better time, daytime but not too hot, we had everything we needed to fix it, it just took a while to unload the truck to get at everything and then get to cranking.

Arrived in Taos needing to replace a spare; drove around town, nobody had one in the right size, off to the opera in someone's backyard - where lambs are raised - with Sang (our hostess), Sara, and Alex. Who has operas in their backyard? With wine and cheese. **Never refuse an invitation.** We went happily, trying something new.

There's a school in town that attracts big talent in the opera world; singers come to the mountain retreat with nothing else to do but study and practice. And give backyard concerts amidst wine, cheese, and unapologetically quirky people who live in Taos. We took it all in and chatted up the singers afterward, eager to understand a foreign scene.

They were profoundly nice, completely immersed in their training, eager to talk about it but also to hear a glimmer of news from the outside world, which we came to represent. I imagined it like the old days when travelers brought word of the latest tales from abroad.

We followed them to dinner and were introduced to Mary Jane Johnson without knowing anything. My first impression proved correct; she was every bit the presence I foresaw. Her first words were said between a big Texas smile: well, you can sit here, but I'm not buying your dinner. Everyone's chairs canted toward her, including mine, and I was sitting right across from her. She spoke on food, people, things, places with a smile and charm that made me like and respect her, and trust her judgment of the students we saw perform and who were sitting around us now.

We shared smiles and swapped stories over burgers served "New Mexico style," chilies all over, and promised to stay in touch, hoping to find a way to cross paths again. And oh yeah, she was nice enough to refuse our contribution to the dinner check.

Spoke to Emily before heading to the opera; she's all over the place, wants me to drop everything and try to fix us, to give her another chance, but won't say it.

She beats me up for all the failings, for the spot that she's in now, for the spot that her family is in, for how bad her life is. For what she doesn't have going for her. I don't know what to think anymore about it all.

In someone's backyard

It's so emotional, she's scheduled to finalize our divorce in court on the 17th.

"I never was a good closer," she said.

I miss her, I miss her terribly, but I wonder if we're meant to be together right now, if she really wants to be with me or just wants a way to get out of her current state. If I'm a least bad alternative.

But by the end we're chatting about normal stuff, GORUCK, her plans to go to DC, Java. Always Java. Looking into another puppy, or at least considering it, for one of us. Or both.

You never know.

Said she would love to just be able to tell Java that we figured out how to work it out.

Me, too. But it might be too late.

June 12 / Taos

San Francisco De Asis / Dennis Hopper's church, where his service was held, was a community service project to renovate. The town rallied together to help fix it up. Teams from SMU were digging for artifacts, carefully, which had nothing to do with Dennis Hopper. But we headed to Dennis Hopper's gravesite, the location of which seemed unknown to most though everyone had ideas on how to get there. We're hypocrites because we hoped it wouldn't turn into a destination grave like Jim Morrison's. It was just so new, and we happened to be in Taos now, and at the church. After much searching, we came across it, a pile of dirt in line with the plot's other rows, still fresh from his life in this world. Mountains, cityscapes, homes true to the landscape and fields of grass all visible, it was serene for its authenticity, for its pile of dirt, for how it was not an homage to Dennis Hopper's life but rather a serene resting spot, unique to him but no more, no less than the rest.

Why were we here?

Visiting gravesites always brings me to my own mortality, to the respect for those who have faced that head on in a way I have not yet had to. For knowing that my father is next, my mother is next, that I pray for an order to it that is natural and lives that are full.

I think of Emily. I think of her father, almost 9 years gone. The pain of sudden death, the pain of natural death. God doesn't give us anything we can't handle in this world. But that doesn't make it easy to deal with when a loved one is considered, when Java is considered - and he only has ten more years, tops - loss is so painful to think about it's a Godsend to be able to focus on our daily lives, on the good, and on the necessary faith to make it through the days of our lives.

Alonso

June 12 / Saturday, Santa Fe

World Cup. USA vs. England starts at 11:30 am. Dropped Alex and Sara downtown, they went to the hotel. I went off and dealt with the car. Oil change, new tires couriered in from Albuquerque led me to the restaurant bar next to the garage. Tortilla Flats, no relation to our Cinco de Mayo spot in NYC - it had the sentimentality of a familiar name a couple thousand miles away, it also had the World Cup game, USA vs. England. When I showed up it was 1-0 England on an early goal. I ate and drank some local and lamented the English lead until we leveled at 1-1. And there it stood.

I don't know how I feel about ties. Lukewarm? Someone should win every game in the World Cup. I don't think Americans get the whole tie concept, and then it goes to some weird point system. Baseball games can go on for hours and hours, extra, to reach a decision. Ties are the most severe form of lukewarm. But if it helps us over there, so be it. If it doesn't, then there should be winners.

Alonso was the man in charge of the car. Two new tires on the rear, two used ones kept on the front, a spare up top and below. His big plans tonight were to hang out with Mike from Ohio, whose brother was bringing some White Lightning from Alabama with him into town. Also known as pure alcohol, moonshine, Alonso said he was eager to talk to Mike's brother for the distillery process techniques. Alonso has the process down until the very end, but then it goes wrong, making a recipe he cannot, as he desires, pass along to his children. These guys are so laid back, have such a good time in the garage, I wished we didn't have to bolt town tonight or I would have tried to figure out a way to try some good ol' Alabama White Lightning. And snag the recipe.

Back to Santa Fe. Worked in a pool hall with Internet on the final posts needed to get the website up and running. Hours and hours of ice water with lemon and a fine-tooth comb looking through pics and captions, layouts and hyperlinks. Formatting.

Chatted with Sara about her enlisting Jack as moral support, her poor judgment. I don't like to micromanage, she likes to be micromanaged. I don't get it, who likes to be micromanaged? But I guess I'll try.

==It's going to get worse, the conditions, the lack of sleep, the pressure, the grind.== And, yet, maybe there's a huge success mounting, a huge motivator just around the corner. But don't count on it.

I tried to bait her into leaving, she said she would if she wanted to, but she doesn't. At all. She was crying, again, about how much she cares about this, how it's the coolest thing she's ever done. I am so emotionally removed from this, to a fault brought on by my personal life, it can be hard to really experience the emotion that this trip requires. It may go down as a legend,

it may be in fact legendary, or it may simply be another adventure, one of many in my life.

Either way, I hope it inspires people as it has Sara. And that they come along for the ride.

The dust is everywhere, in the car, on the car, in my eyes. Yet it's a nice day, not at all windy, mild temperatures, but my skin is drying out, my eyes in constant need of a prolonged blink. Is it like this all the time? Reminds me of the desert, which, I suppose makes sense.

#10 at The Shed, in the courtyard lit up with light strings and the constant backdrop of live music coming from a bar nearby - wherever you are in town. On recommendation from an old buddy.

Chili sauce on point, if you like that kind of thing. When in Santa Fe, I love it. I opted to get mine red and green instead of Christmas so that I could taste the difference.

When it arrived, I ate it too quickly to really make a note of which I liked better. It was all good, perfect with a local Santa Fe Ale - the only meal I'd choose before getting in the car and driving four hours to Alamogordo for an early morning jump into White Sands in soft light.

June 13 / Drive from Santa Fe -> Alamogordo, NM then -> White Sands

Sara complaining once we were close, around 230 in the morning, just to stop anywhere. Since I drove the entire way, all 4 and a half hours, I found it a bit annoying. I asked Alex how he wanted to get the shot, at what time. 630 wake up from the motel 8 where we were. Left by 7 after I got coffee and breakfast for them, at White Sands by 730. Drove around an 8-mile loop we should have run.

Ran into a French guy who carried a camera and tripod and complained about the light. His wife read Madame Bovary in the car parking lot while he ran around for pictures.

The dunes were cool, not all what I expected though. Their location, the way they formed, made them special.

Under a missile launch testing facility and close to the LBJ NASA landing site, it seemed a bit governmental for the typical National Park. Still very cool. Much better with no shoes on. We were free to slalom up and down the dunes.

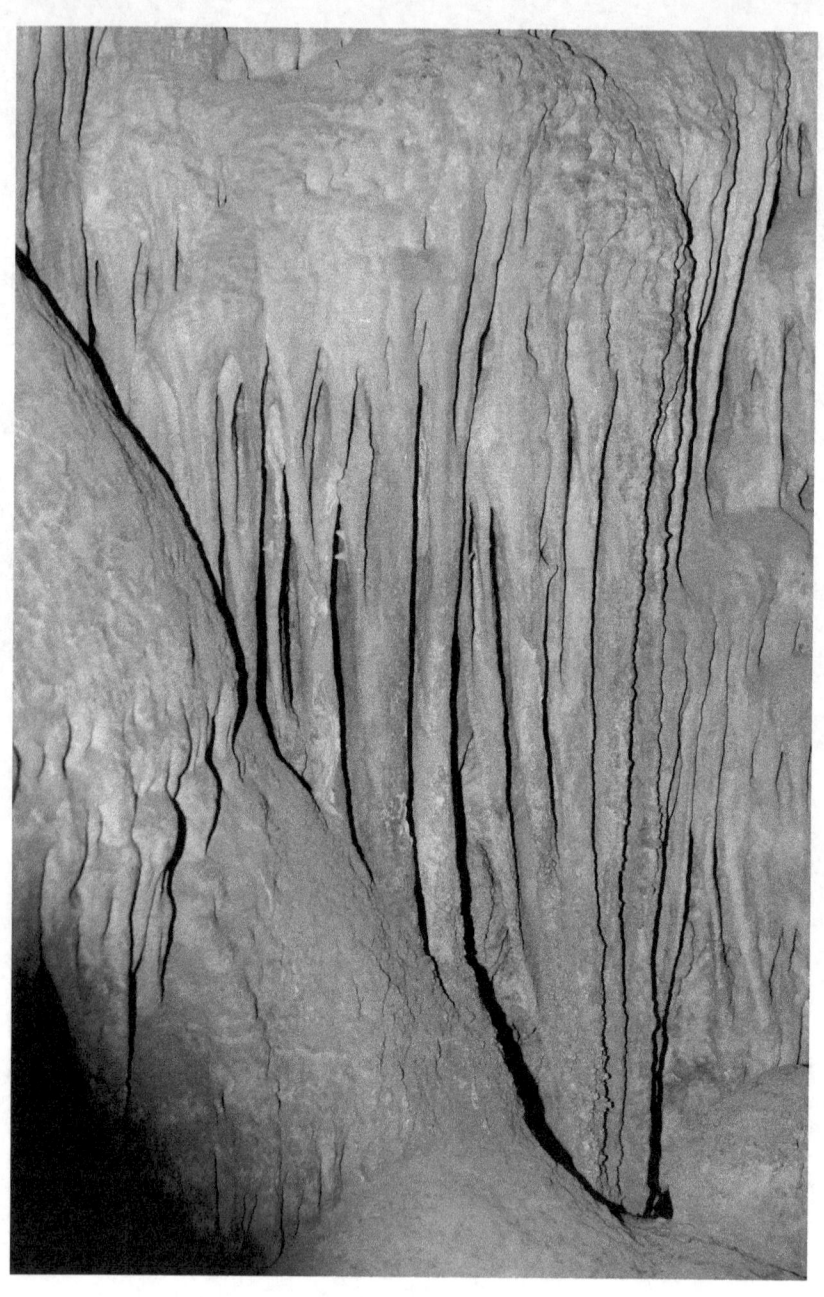

A boring picture of the rocks

June 14 / Arizona

The trip to Tucson on 2 hours sleep was long, and felt longer. The cacti everywhere were cool in a not so polished as a postcard kind of way, the scenery kept me going. It's been a while since we've been out West. It all seemed new again. Stopped at the Colossal Cave Mountain Park, got to chatting with a guy at the entrance, Van, and left the tour of the Cave to Alex and Sara. ==I can talk about anything west of the Mississippi, he said, so I let him.==

Van, A Marriott executive chef, retired at 36 when the getting was really good, to focus on his true passion: people. And their stories. When I asked about the stories his hat must hold, it turned out I was right. The hat belonged to Larry Mahan, a championship bull rider. I asked more specifically about the silver band, and Van smiled, saying that bands were like belt buckles and boots - unique to the cowboy. His was silver. And one of a kind, traded in Lajitas, TX for a full meal out of the back of his car with a guy who was completely broke and looking to keep pushing south. Cowboy etiquette: east of the Mississippi a cowboy always removes his hat at dinner or indoors, otherwise anything goes. It just depends. Van loved people, he loves educating people, and he loves to educate himself about other people, what they do and why. Smiles go a very, very long way, and he has this figured out to a hilt.

Went to meet Mich and Wendy in their place in the northern part of town, resting above Tucson. The roof deck was just the slice of heaven we needed. Beers and a clock that dragged on and on as we all got more and more tired, a sunset that lasted forever and made me think of Emily's dad, whose family was from Tucson. In fact, Emily's family was all over my thoughts coming here. We were always supposed to visit Tucson together, it just never happened, like so many other things. And I wished she would have been here with me now, just to share the memories, to add meaning to the trip I now feel I am making alone. And not just in Tucson. So we drove around town, checked out U of A, artsy shops around town and a quiet Sunday downtown deserted. It was a bit solemn for me, knowing how this would all be so emotional for Emily were she here. I imagine I'll always think of her when I think of so many things, Tucson and its sunsets among them.

June 15 / Tucson, AZ -> San Diego, CA

Wake-up on Mich's deck up top, slept gloriously - sunlight peeking over the eastern mountains.

Ran the Phone Line Trail with Alex, wished still very much that Em would have been there to run with me, with us, to share this adventurous yet safe part of my life. The trail itself was legit and raised above the rest of the trails around there. The elevation reminded me of Colorado when I first moved out there. You just have to be used to it, which I was not. The first part was really tough, up some barely marked trails to switchbacks to get to elevation. Snakes were lingering around here and there no doubt, though I didn't see any. They say it's the second person in the file that gets bit after the first stirs it. I hate snakes. But up we went to the top, the distance was just under 10 miles.

We met Bryce, the senior to be at West Point, who is from here. Wrapped up at Mich's - he was gone to work by the time we got back. We jumped in his pool and enjoyed the air, with its hot sun, before packing up and hitting the road.

Drove to San Diego. To Rancho to see Julie, no Internet after Alex took some stupid pics of her new model buddy she wants to manage. Drama.

Alex to the lodge to work. Sara woke up at 1030, didn't make her bed, Julie called me later to say she thought Sara just didn't have what it takes. I slept horribly, worried about Alex at the inn backdating everything, and pissed about the pictures Julie made him take.

Small earthquake in the night, rocking the chandeliers at the lodge. So small it didn't register on the news.

Road Fuel

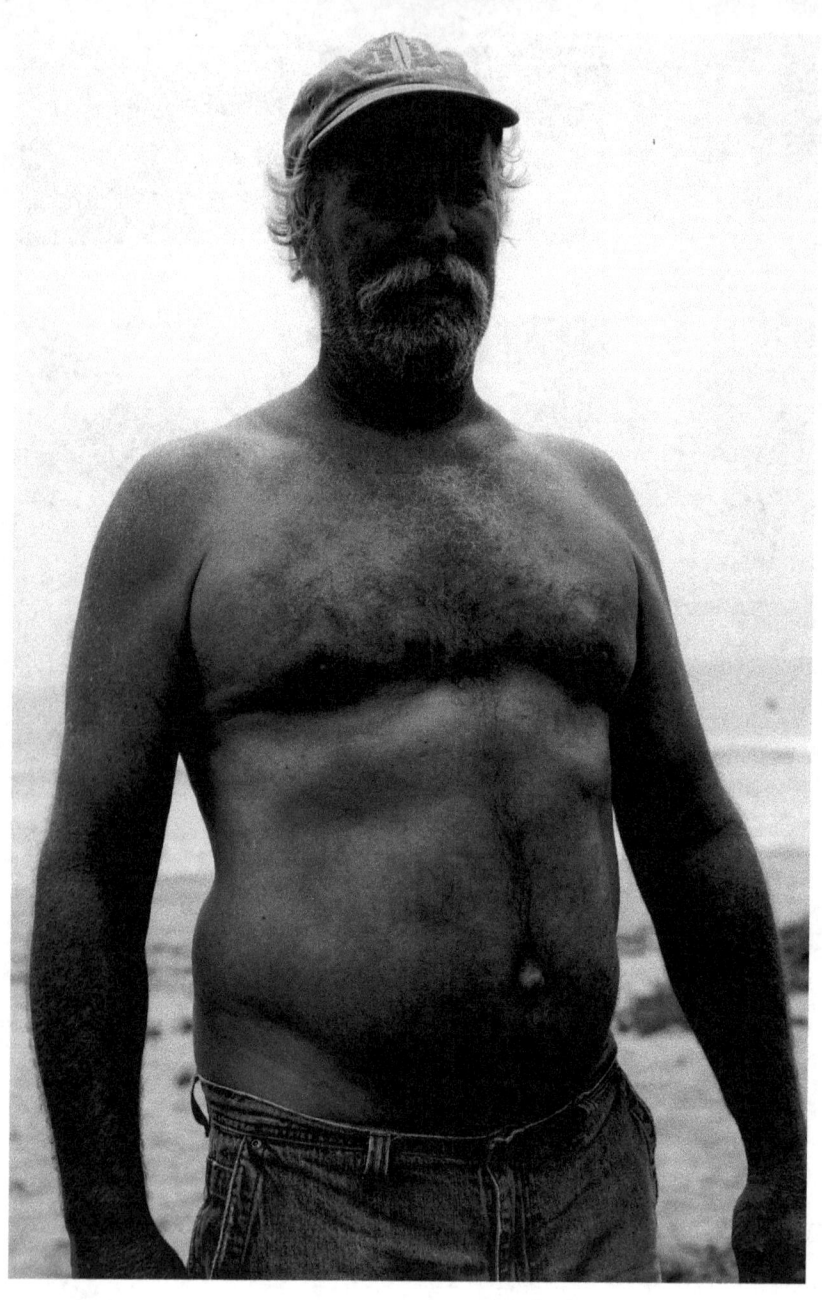

Mark

June 16 / The Point, San Diego

Wanted to hang out and check out the surf scene in SD; as a can-barely-surf' kind of guy who didn't want to mess with the 'locals only' mantra, it was still a blast just to check out, and I'm not one for spectator sports unless it's college football or something.

Mark and his friends invited us over for some beers and dogs after jokingly asking me where I was from. Implication: not from around here. The camera probably gave me away, or do I just smile differently than everyone on the West Coast? We joked around for a while and he told us some of his stories, we told him some of ours, we talked to Brian, who was 6 months away from basic training for the Navy to be a medic. I told him it would change him, always for the better, and that he should have as much fun as he can while he's doing it. I wish I had considered the military sooner in life. Brian was straight out of high school, surfing in the meantime.

I wish I would have gone to West Point and graduated in May of 2001 as an Infantry Officer.

A meeting with ▮▮▮▮ at No Fear. He wants to sell a t-shirt to everyone every six months for the rest of their lives. He is in the commodity business, opening up his own stores because wholesale is a bad, bad business to be in. Branding takes time, there is no substitute. He wants to be everywhere, so he's opening up his own retail store.

Yeah...wholesale is an awful business to be in. Too much inventory costs to carry bags, Ogio is the leader because they are quality for the price. Ubiquity. Not GORUCK, I'd rather be smaller, fewer places. Beck Boots, the Klausmeyer Dairy, the Agassi School.

Start small and get it right, put blood sweat and tears into it.

Built in the USA, not shipped off to China to be made cheaper & more disposable. I challenge the assumption that people really want more stuff, it's clutter now. There are enough people out there who want quality, who will pay for it, who will know it when they see it.

Mariachi

To LA.

Stopped at Mariachi Plaza just to get out of the car, walked around, ate a street taco, loaded back up.

Carpool service for Alex and Sara, never an enviable task for anyone in LA. People drive there, that's what they do. It's not for me like that, but besides that I was slightly intrigued by how much I liked LA, driving around once the traffic died down. The last time I was there, just before I joined the Army, I was on the verge of doing something that made it difficult for me to just be normal. I needed that step but it took a little bit of time to get there, so I passed it in LA. It's not the best place to find yourself, but if you've already got it, it's a nice place.

Met up with Alia, who I last saw 15 years ago in Florida. Facebook. She's one of the locals there now, she's been there so long, and seems uncomfortably comfortable there. She's still waiting for her break but enjoying just being there. It's home now.

We caught up over a couple beers at her boyfriend's bar, an LA place I liked infinitely more after the owner, Micah, described how he painted the walls and built the fixtures himself 6 years ago. Behind LA there are still men & women who build things and take pride in them. A practice that becomes their lives, that they take pride in.

Said goodbye to Alia, snapped a picture for the moms, and headed to Chinny's in Brentwood. Got there late, he talked about his job, we talked about GORUCK. Goes without saying that we fall seamlessly back into each other's lives. There are so few people like that in my life, that I can talk to about anything, even at midnight on a weekday showing up at his place, chatting for a couple hours before he heads back to negotiate contracts for his clients, Jerry McGuire style. He's a good egg, Chinny.

June 16 / Driving to Las Vegas

Early wake-up, working in Chinny's kitchen all morning, I left him a couple rucks and wished I had more time.

Driving to Vegas, meeting at Andre Agassi's school on Thursday with Marcia. Beautiful drive from LA to Vegas once we got out of the traffic.

Open roads, desert air, lights of Vegas appear slightly dim these days, the town empty. But we didn't even really drive through, it was mostly just a feeling.

Into Henderson, no Internet, bolt for the Holiday Inn Express to use the Internet all night.

Meeting Agassi in the morning.

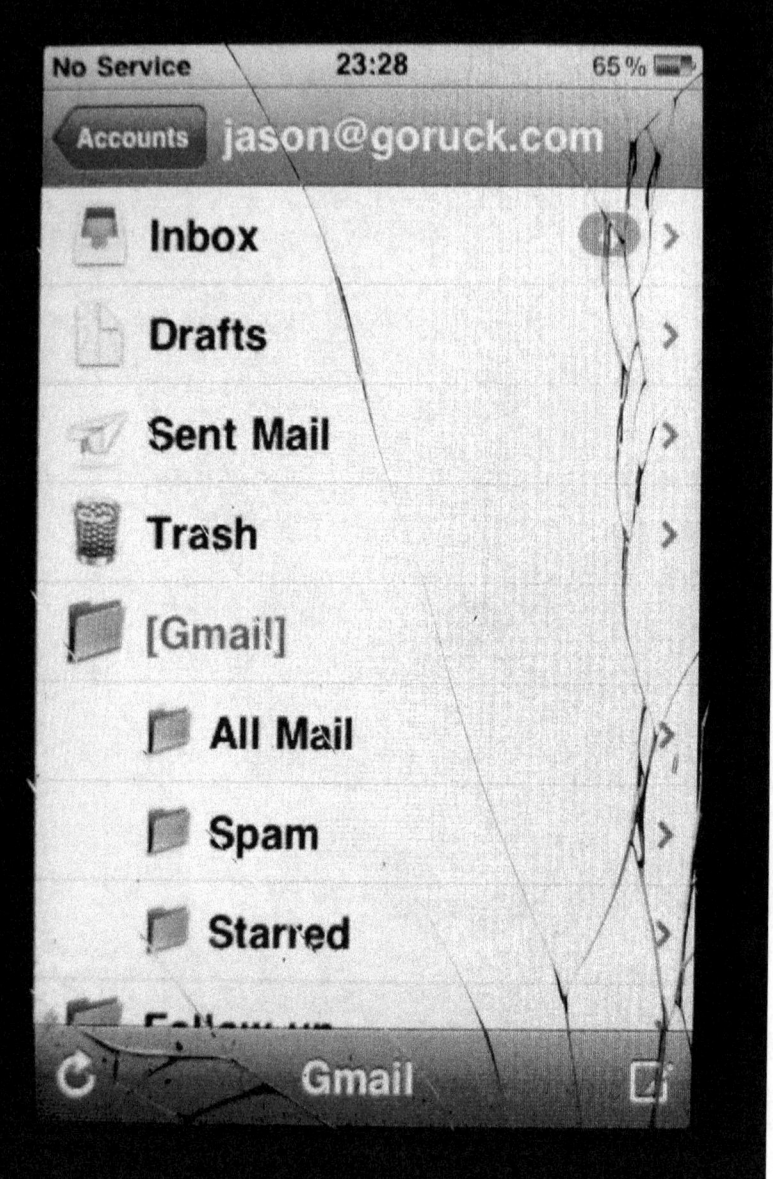

4 emails, no service, and a cracked screen

>>> On Wed, Jun 16, 2010 at 1:33 PM, Emily <██████████@gmail. com >>> Subject: Re: Consent Final Judgment > >>> wrote: >>>> >>>> jase. i just got a call from the lawyer's office. apparently you were supposed to review this consent final judgement and sign it and return it with a wet signature. stephanie just told me they did not have this document signed by you on file. there can be no court date tomorrow but she said if you overnight it, i can still get a court date for this friday with the same judge. otherwise it is wait until july 6. i don't know what else to say at this point.

>> On Jun 16, 2010, at 8:35 PM, Jason McCarthy >> <██████████@ gmail.com> >> wrote: two things, 1) i'm in the middle of nowhere right now. the desert, literally. 2) the address in the document is wrong, it's back as the Murray whatever address. please advise. >>> --jason

> On Wed, Jun 16, 2010 at 12:23 PM, Emily <██████████@gmail. com> > wrote: >> And no need to be short with me I'm never going to be your business partner. No matter what.

On Jun 16, 2010, at 9:29 PM, Jason McCarthy <██████████@gmail. com> wrote: > you're right, i'm sorry. it's like when you get in the mode of speaking a different language it can be hard to transition over. i'm sorry. yes, i'll meet with you. of course. i may be in jax in a few days. aren't you already my business partner, sort of ;) ok, i'll stop with that. how do you feel about calling ginger and seeing what her puppy situation is? i love you, you know, i wish there were more i could do to help. > xoxojase

From: Emily <██████████@gmail.com> Date: Wed, Jun 16, 2010 at 5:55 PM Subject: Re: Consent Final Judgment To: Jason McCarthy <██████████@gmail.com> You know, I wrote that and sent it and was like, well shit...technically... Ha still you understand me and know how 'please advise' ruffles my feathers. I understand your stress and the language barriers so to speak. About the puppy situation, let's just play it by ear. Love you too, always will no matter. Be safe. Java is on a 5 lick program w me these days, he's so smart but is not pleased w his moms idea of optimal sleeping temp. Nor am I for that matter. F this iPhone keyboard I'm out of practice.

Marcia

June 17 / Las Vegas / Agassi School

The nervousness all morning of wondering if Vegas was on West Coast time. My iphone said it was, but I still hate relying on that thing to give me everything from directions to the time, for storing my data, for almost making me dependent.

We showed up to the school around 930 on the north side of town, sort of nervous about being there, not because of Andre, but because there was no good reason to show up when school was out of session except that we happened to be there then. The week before President Clinton and Senator Harry Reid were there to promote the school's good work, which was, ummmm, the same reason why we were there.

Marcia, the Chancellor of the school, greeted us with the type of smile and firm handshake that made me think that she was both compassionate and competent, demanding and understanding. The types of balances I have historically overextended. Marcia got nervous when we asked to mic her up, and had to make a call, which was exactly when Andre popped his head into the office. I happily gave them creative control over everything, explaining that the focus was overwhelmingly positive and meant to be really well done, to focus on the people who work there and their lives, how they take pride in their jobs and in helping people. If they don't like what we come up with, and they will, that's on us. Andre is an easy focal point, but he's not right for us to focus on this time. So Marcia gave us a tour at the expense of a meeting she said she preferred not to attend, and she showed us everything and introduced us to everyone who came across our path.

==There was no fear of the boss in anyone's eyes, there was only a community of people really set out to make a difference in kids' lives.==

Chatted with Andre for a while, everything came up except the bags, which is better for the occasion. The focus was the school, so we chatted on education, how he has achieved the success, his managerial skills, and lack of skills in really driving the train forward, but that he is a good figurehead for the cause. Sara and Alex really liked him, thought he was 'the man'. I kinda knew what to expect, that he was the nicest guy ever, slightly stung by getting the short end of a few sticks. I saw it when he asked me for creative control, even though it went without saying that any type of less than stellar light would have made things with Julie, who set it all up, awkwardly not the right answer. I talked about the Army, exchange years in Heidelberg. Andre talked about his school kids going to France, looking at bringing on an exchange student, big ideas that he has for the school.

I liked talking to him, he didn't really seem like anyone but the guy next door, and then he invited me to his next event to raise money for the school. And the $400 million he helped raise for Philadelphia schools.

"If you can believe, You can achieve"

Got in the car, headed to Holiday Inn Express, sat there till about 6pm, ate their happy hour dinner, spoke to Emily about why I didn't do anything right when she called me up, frantic about her health insurance premiums.

It's just back to the same old deal where we don't make decisions well together, where the expectations on me are so high, still, to do everything right by us, but there is probably a reason why we are where we are, as tragically sad as that makes me.

So we drive to the Hoover Dam, whose efficiency makes it boring despite its size. Yet the people come and the people go to see it in action. Well, minus the action, they come to see its size because it's on the way to wherever they're going. And it's worth seeing. For the efficient way it does what it does.

Ranger TV

June 18 / Grand Canyon

Arrived at the Grand Canyon campsite just past midnight, we had charcoal for a fire, no wood, it's me at my most patient around a campfire. There's just something about it that garners the respect of all, from our ancestors until now.

It feels like magic to start a fire and get it going, to stand around and stare at its power, to feel its heat. And so it's one of the few things in this world that inspires patience from me. I was in a down mood, dealing with Emily, and Sara who wants to be micromanaged at a time when I'm not capable of micromanaging one more thing. I just can't.

Alex came over and said "I'm just gonna say it, I got tons of work too bro, but you gotta just have a few beers and relax". I'm just not here right now, man, I said in response. I got to making the fire, lots of blowing right into it, and eventually got it going. I had a few beers, and passed out in my bag next to the coals, full from two sausages and an ear of corn.

While all was not right in the world, I slept peacefully and woke up feeling better.

June 19 / Grand Canyon -> 89 to Sundance

9 years since Emily's father died, 3 years since my first big mission in Iraq. Em wrote me to say she hasn't come very far at all, that she's broken. I feel responsible. I feel I could have done more to help her, to help us. I wish I could go back and change so much.

I don't think there is anything, on this earth, more important than the one you love. And so I have so much figured out, but that remains a mystery.

Tore down the tent, I was pretty silent all morning, something I'm getting used to being, packed everything up and headed for the main attraction.

A short distance from our campsite, it was hard to believe that the colossal Grand Canyon was so close. There was an annoying amount of construction going on around the visitors center, walking around roped off area after roped off area. I felt like a lazy, spoiled brat for complaining. We saw something peek through the trees in the distance, but it didn't make sense to us. And then we were there, standing right on top of it.

No picture can do it justice, the size, its grandeur. Imagining yourself wandering upon it for the first time and thinking that it is simply the most extraordinary piece of land you've ever seen.

No words. Barely any pictures.

Then we drove up 89, heading to Sundance, several pictures of ledges with horses in the foreground.

Powell Lake. Memories of summertime with my dad: drive to a lake, camp out, take the boat out, water ski, find girls to play spin the bottle with while the grown ups drink and grill out. Horseshoes, ATVs. Simpler, easier fun, low maintenance with smiles that aren't as existential as they can be.

Arrived in Sundance for a late dinner at Uncle John's house. Friday night. John was passed out in his chair, disoriented.

So Buck (his dog) was our main greeter.

Alex and I worked at the kitchen table, Sara made food. Then she went to her room and we didn't see her until Alex went and asked if she really made dinner just for herself and then left.

So she came over and made something for us while we worked.

Had a conversation about the News section of the website, and what we wanted to call it. We wanted to flesh out ideas on whether store placements or things like that were News.

Sundance, Utah

We said we didn't want to overdo the store side of it, that we don't want to appear small.

Sara kept not getting it, then didn't get why we wouldn't want to store consumer data of users at our site.

Privacy issues will crush us if we were ever to get caught doing something like that, plus I just don't feel right doing that stuff. So we won't.

I said 'whatever' when we had to keep repeating ourselves over and over and went back to working online, headphones in.

Cache #2 — Finders Keepers

GR Cache #2

GORUCK fan —

Thanks for hunting GORUCK gear in one of the most beautiful places in the country. Please send us a picture and a story to cache@goruck.com
You rock!

Jason

20 June 2010
Sundance, UT
Amphitheater

June 19 Sundance, UT

Wake-up pretty early in the AM after chatting with John for a couple hours in the middle of the night. Down to check it out with Alex, we walked around a bit and then went for a run that turned into quite a long one. I did a Cache at the amphitheater, then we ran to Stewart Falls, passing by hikers, yogis, bikers, and generally really happy people.

It was gorgeous, reminding me why this is a truly special place for me. A bit secluded, but not too much. Outdoorsy but still comfortable, and the Owl Bar is there. The type of bar you feel classy to be in because it's in Sundance and it's about being in Sundance. Ran around Aspen Grove before heading back to the house, hung out with John, too exhausted to do anything but sit on the couch and relax until Alex said he didn't want to just sit around and watch golf on TV while in Sundance.

Sara was sick with 'altitude sickness' so she stayed behind. We stood outside under the pines, grilled a quick dinner, and then headed down to the Owl Bar. Two beers and some blues rock.

Hung out with the band a bit, loved the atmosphere here. Burn barrel outside was a new find for me. A fire in the woods at night. Back up the mountain, passed out.

My dad & Leslie entering
Wyoming — 1999

June 20 / Sunday / Sundance, UT -> Flaming Gorge, WY

Not much doing in Sundance besides listening to John babble about his hangouts with Brad Pitt and Apolo Ohno, watching some of the World Cup. We headed out.

It became a driving afternoon, on our way to Flaming Gorge, Wyoming.

I don't know why, but something about entering the Cowboy State had me absolutely thrilled. Driving alongside the sunset, watching the scenery go by at 75mph was a moving panoramic of beauty.

Dark mountains silhouetting the sky still light, albeit barely, past 10pm. Trees along the ridgeline, we made our way to Lucerne campsite, got a fire going, ate some sausages and drank some beer, and I fell asleep next to the fire. Full moon on the still waters of the Green River.

June 21 / Flaming Gorge, WY

Starting to feel that my biggest challenge is in reducing my expectations of the people around me. To trust them.

I hate reducing my standards and it's hard for me to trust right now, so I rely on myself.

I need less sleep than them, I can last longer than them, and I have the perspective of thinking that everything we do here is pretty luxurious.

I don't need nice hotels, or even a tent for that matter.

I just need to be able to get my stuff done, some time to myself in the mornings (preferably with coffee), and to be loved.

Sleeping on the road

June 22 / Steamboat Springs / Tuesday

Em is having a breakdown, we traded 100 or so text messages, I am at a total loss but I'm removed from the world she's in, what am I supposed to do? Is there anything I can do? I just wish she had found someone to make her happy, that she was right when she wanted to be right, I wish I could remove the past because she is THE ONE.

Driving from Steamboat to Boulder to catch the end of Jason Fell's softball game. Is there anything we don't find interesting? Haha. Working in Steamboat after a mosquito-filled wake-up followed by utter relaxation at the Strawberry Springs. All ten minutes that I was able to relax, that is. I feel like I have so much going on. Is this my fate to always be so high strung, brain churning?

Ice cream shop in a small town gas station en route. Delicious mocha malt, it came recommended. And we were off on our way again shortly. Have to talk to Sara, our working relationship is souring, she's running everything through Alex, I don't want to tell her to do anything, and I don't trust that she knows GORUCK. Or me for that matter, and it's very uncomfortable, distractingly so.

Just in time for the softball slaughter, saw Dana and caught up with the Fells briefly. Quick bite with the whole crew, Jack showed up + Dana at West End, got a burger, it was good to sit outside on the patio. Sara seems increasingly like she's sitting at the edge of the table, not sharing in the story, the camaraderie, because she just doesn't get it, she's not really part of the team. My fault for not training her more, but after 6 weeks on the road with me, she has had enough time to get it, to start to piece things together that she can do. Her talents are enormous, she's just still on the outside.

Awkward figuring out sleeping situations, Alex went with Sara to the Fell's, Jack and I went to Dana's and stayed up far later than either of us wanted to, discussing what to do with Sara. Though somewhat receptive to the idea of keeping her around in some capacity, we both agreed that in the truck with me was not the right place for her, and that we didn't really know what was the right place for her to be, so it's becoming difficult for us to want to keep her on at all when we barely know how she can translate her skills. I've known her for 15 years and it's becoming increasingly hard to imagine having her leave, but it's not working out. I really like her, but it's not working out, and I don't feel that great about it.

We had so much to think about

and so few answers.

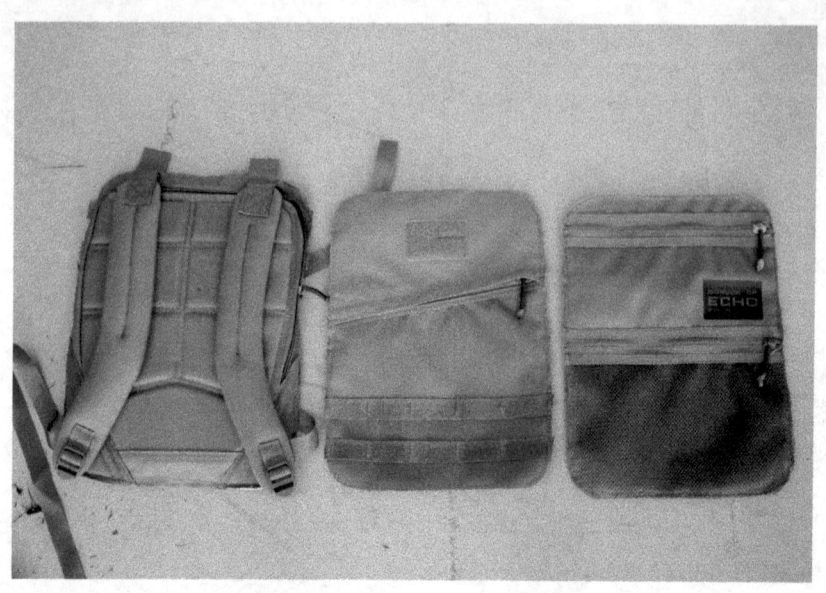

June 23 / Boulder, CO / Wednesday

Bike to Work Day. Jack and I went to Moe's on Broadway to check out the scene. Bikers everywhere enjoying the sense of community, the free food, and, in a random bar here and there, the early morning USA World Cup game. I waited around uncomfortably to talk to Sara, at least briefly, before heading to our factory, but they were running late so it had to get postponed.

At Colorado Bag Co all day, controlling the quality, which usually means that I'm rejecting most of everything for this reason or that. It sucks, but they can't get us where we need to go, so we'll have to go somewhere else.

I really like them, too, but - as it will be with Sara - it's a painful goodbye.

Jack and I got to downtown Denver to meet up with Sara and Alex and go to the Rockies game. Jack and I watched the first couple innings in a one pool table kind of local bar across from the stadium, then met our other half in front and headed in. A great game, a lot of fun, and the Rockies hit a walk-off home run in the bottom of the 9th to win.

We were thrilled, thinking that the town would come to life after a win like this. By and large we were right, and Denver showed us a great time.

Got into a huge fight with Sara at the second car, where she said she was fine to drive, I said there was no way she was driving my car, which I was responsible for, after drinking. The exasperation extended into appeals to Alex and Jack as to what she was supposed to say to something like that, to which I replied that she should say absolutely nothing for a change. For a change.

Back to the hotel, she bolted out of the car, then whistled when we pulled around. I told Alex, after he asked, that she wasn't going to be coming along with us anymore, he told me I had better talk to her now or he'd be really pissed at me. I was going to wait till morning, but off I went.

Do you want to talk now or in the morning? - the morning - well I want to talk now. This is unacceptable led to should I pack my bags led to yes.

She came in my room later, got the keys, packed her stuff up, and then wanted to talk about it, which consisted of an hour or so of her telling me how great she was. I said that tonight was a colossal loss of judgment, that we didn't work well together, that neither of us was happy working with the other, and that I was sorry it didn't work out because I really liked her. And she really likes me, too. She wanted to work in other areas of the company, to which I said there were no other areas besides what we were doing, all together in the car, in the fucking grind.

Cut it up

After saying that it was my job to teach her GORUCK, I prodded her to say that she wasn't sorry for anything all summer, that she was just being herself.

Which led to me saying that the teaching was over and that I was sorry, that it was us, not me, not her, but us.

She left.

I tried to read the Rolling Stone article on McCrystal getting fired and fell asleep in the bed before Jack and Alex came back from their drinkathon across the street.

I didn't feel like joining them.

Look at all the fun I missed.

Rope Swing, Boulder Creek

June 24 / Boulder, CO / Thursday

Got the tour of Moe's in the morning, the first in a long while without Sara, felt relieved but still a bit bad about the whole ordeal. It didn't make me happy, I wasn't glad to get rid of her, to send her wherever she went, but it was necessary.

She believed in the brand so much but unfortunately that didn't mean that she was a good fit for it. The next time I hire someone I'll have them bring their running shoes and tell me about how they have thrived in the best and the worst team environments. I'll be a bit smarter about it.

Jack and Alex still hungover, we went to Boulder Creek, nobody wanted to jump in or anything. Went back to town, worked all day, had lunch with Dana, who got dumped via email (who does that?), and I went out into town at night to meet up with Dana and her friend - while Jack and Alex went to some hotel on the outskirts.

GR2 Loadout

June 25 / Boulder, CO -> Pikes Peak / Friday

Jack and I back to the Colorado Bag Co factory while Alex went to check out some climbers.

More problems with the bags, but they're getting better, maybe, slowly. Order fulfillment out of their factory only after we've signed off on every bag that they make.

To the Springs, to Josh's. Herding cats to get everyone there. We hung out for a while getting ready, loading our stuff. Watching the rain clouds come in. Corey showed up and we met Brian and Blake at the Pikes Peak trailhead. Up we went, took me back.

The campsite was incredibly nice. We stopped halfway for some water - iodine tablets - and to take a breath. Ate some bread inside, there were campers galore just hanging out in there, we were reasonably tired but wanted to make it to A-Frame to have a little bit more room to ourselves. We pressed on, the darkness started to creep in and we were off the trail before you knew it. So we wandered around, found but not lost, and came across the A-Frame.

We hunted firewood down, threw boulders at logs. Campfire with Josh and the boys was a dream, left me longing for the good old days when I knew how good I had it with them. Yet I longed for Emily by my side.

And now I have neither, or both, in their right place, but somehow I miss them both.

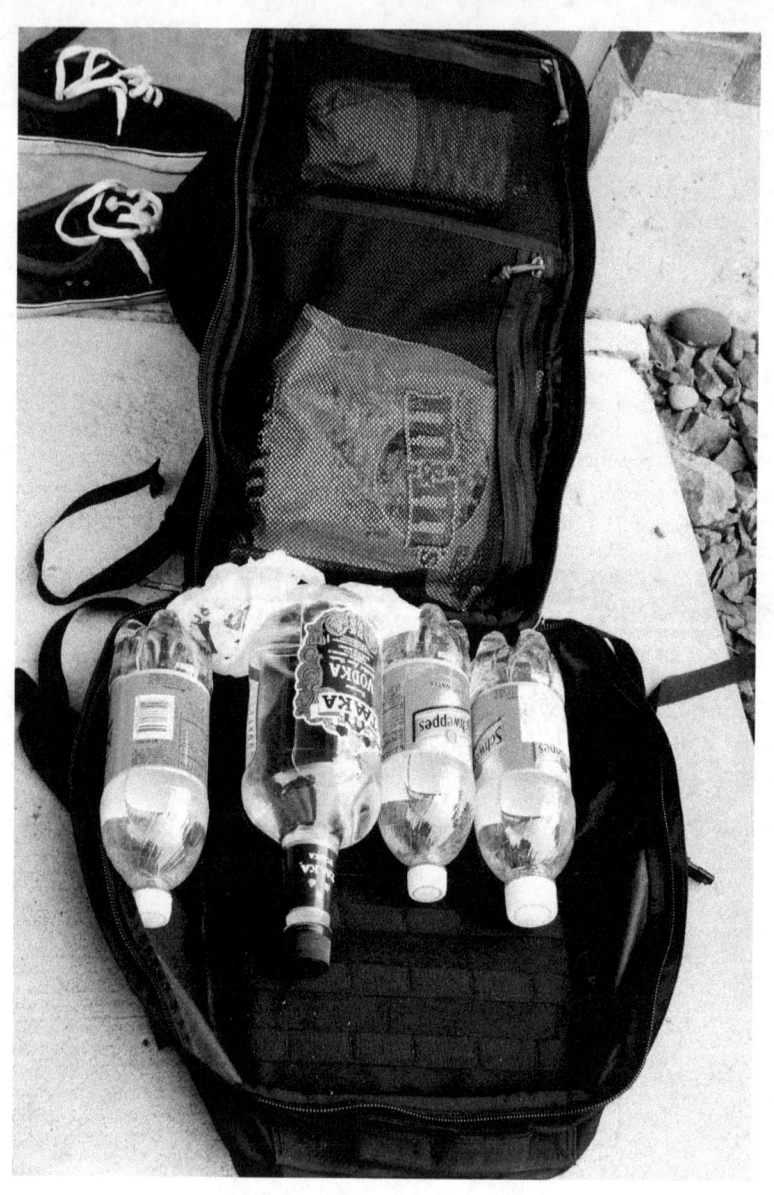

Peanut M&M's,
Vodka Tonic —

All the essentials

Dudes I love —
I need to make more time for adventures like this

Pikes Peak Summit

June 26 / Colorado Springs -> Fort Collins, CO / Saturday

Left for the summit around 10, got there, took pics, took the cog railway down. Back to Josh's, left around 5 or so, up to Fort Collins after checking out the Garden of the Gods. Went downtown, felt a little bit like a frat house city, couple beers, local, to bed.

June 27 / Fort Collins, CO -> Omaha, NE / Sunday

Woke up, worked, went to the Brewers Festival but couldn't drink because of the drive ahead, so it was a bit lame. **Like a corpse standing on a dance floor.** We had the real deal up Pikes Peak so this was payback. Could have been awesome. Left for Omaha, drove 7 hrs, got to the Drover just before closing at 10pm, ate a great meal, chatted with the locals and Skip the manager, loved the place. Whiskey Ribeye. Loved it even though it was fattier than I usually like. Back to a Ramada with great Internet, up till 4am working, slept in cold air and, this time, clean air, not in the least bit musty like we've grown used to at all these non-descript motels across the country.

Road Fuel

June 28 / Omaha -> Iowa City, IA / Monday

Up late, like 11am, stayed at the Ramada till about 1230, headed out to Iowa City to meet up with John's friend Dan after stopping by Rosenblatt Stadium. A bit flat but early still, there was a buzz yet to come. Stopped at a ton of gas stations for Alex to photo the coffee stations. Kum and Go, you name it we stopped there. Iowa City around 8, walked around with Dan, grabbed Mexican outside, played pool to watch the College World Series, went back and passed out, relieved we didn't need to play game to a host hell-bent on creating an adventure.

A blowdryer never looked so good

June 29 / Iowa -> Chicago / Tuesday

Iowa 80 en route to Taste of Chicago, Cubs game with Joe, back to Joe's after dinner south with him. He's a character, a bit over the top. Doesn't drink anymore but he dips, smokes cigars and weed, and drives really really fast through town. Greeted us with a white polo and a cigar outside Wrigley, loud and boisterous, repeatedly talking about Tommy boy, our mutual friend. The privileged by something type.

June 30 Wed / Chicago Straight Shot -> Atlanta

Early wake-up, airport to drop off Alex.

<mark>On my own again.</mark> Drive to Atlanta through Louisville. 12 hours straight through.

Ali museum closed, went to Louisville Slugger museum instead, on to Nashville. Waiting on the Wizard of Oz to start at the Parthenon. Energy was electric in Nashville, people all over the place just to be around an event like movie in the park. Last week was rained out, tonight was a perfect night for just about anything. It seems like forever since I lived in Nashville, but I remember it fondly. I remember the Parthenon and West End above all, plus my friends I haven't stayed in touch with, but it feels like a familiar place along the way. Even though I don't run into anyone I know it feels like a town that used to be home. So I head down to the West End to check it out, there's live music everywhere, kind of like Austin only with a Nashville flare. I suppose you could say Austin is like Nashville but with an Austin flare. Check it out, load up on coffee and head to Atlanta.

Driving in the dark, led by yellow lines, wasn't much of a problem tonight. It all seemed laid out before me, very organized, there were enough trucks on the road to make it seem busy enough and not desolate and not too many to seem crowded. Atlanta, on the other hand, was emptier than the highways. Rolled into an empty town and headed straight for an oldie but a goodie, the Majestic Diner. It lived up to my memory of it, with stuff going on (but not too much on account of the day of the week), the people there were all - or had been at least - up to something, looking to waste the very end of a night that should have ended hours ago. And there I was, talking to Brian, the waiter, who has been there for two years and loves it, manages to do whatever he wants with the rest of his life and though slightly awkward (who isn't at that hour I guess?) seems comfortably so, at least as much as possible.

July 1 / Atlanta, GA / MLK Museum

Slept in the car just up the street from the Majestic - I was just too tired to search around for a hotel at 4 in the morning, get woken up by cleaning staff and people with more 'normal' schedules etc. So I gutted it out in the early hours, after a wake-up around 8am, and headed to the MLK museum. Shamefully, despite going to college in Atlanta, I had never been and thought it important to see with my own two eyes. Though not the most beautiful building I've ever been to, nor the most high-tech, nor the one most suitable to accommodate the number of visitors it should receive, the message was spread as powerfully as any other because of the people who came to visit, the people who were there There was an ultimate respect stemming from a belief that so much was owed to the man who now rests on the grounds, with his wife, both of whom paid such a price for that respect. It was awe, love, gratitude, and pride that emanated from the grounds to all who visit.

Drove all afternoon through Georgia to get home.

There is no place like home, broken as it is for me now, haunted as it is for me now, with Emily hanging out at her mom's house, 30 minutes and 3 million miles away. In the same town after so many months of not being so, of being so far away so I could pretend at least that she was too far away. And yet a home cooked meal still tastes better at home, so it was good to be there.

3:22 am time stamp
Curled up in the passenger seat trying to fall asleep
Tave in the back, panting
Had to run the A/C to fall asleep.

July 2 / Jacksonville / Home in Florida

Got Swizzle to do some product photos with a white background. Not his normal restaurant food gig, but better than nothing. Price was right.

To Sliders for dinner, an oldie but a goodie, for oysters not yet saturated in oil from the spill. A perfect night, dinner with my mom is always good though taking pictures and walking around a place I've been going to for years feels a little bit different than a new place discovered for the first time. Because it's such an institution, Sliders holds so many memories for me.

The day spent mostly by the computer, mostly just hanging out, working, trying to catch up but lost in thoughts of every other time I've been back, of how different it is now than it used to be.

And so while I am myself at home more than anywhere else, myself is more scarred, more bruised here than elsewhere, so being home is tough.

Firecracker 400

July 3 / Daytona Beach, FL

Headed to Daytona for the race, an all day event. Mike and I had pit passes so we walked around on this overcast day we were pretty sure would pose a threat to the start time. This race felt so different than Indy, much more of a family event here, but equally as many smiles to go around. The turns were steeper than I could have possibly imagined, and as people wandered around and spilled cocktails on the track, and signed the start line, I wondered if there was any risk to that kind of stuff on a track where cars go around it at however fast they go, 200mph or something. I had a blast though the day was a long one, thankfully broken up by showers until they caused a two-hour delay. Night racing is way cool, though, and I'm thrilled to have seen it, and the fans who love it.

July 4 / Jacksonville, FL

I had a simple, easy day in mind, worn out from the Firecracker 400 festivities, the travel, the emotional grind of being back in Florida.

Emily became a godmother today, Johnny's little boy, Andrew.

I was really happy for her, knowing full well how big of a deal it is.

And yet what an inadequate substitute it will be for her given the kids she has wanted so badly for so long. And yet knowing that this was no substitute.

I hung out at Mike's in Ormond for the day, slightly off.

Mostly just worn out but excited to see Emily the next day, nervous but excited.

In the meantime, the excitement from the 4th - I worked but not really, mostly just distracted and missing Java and Emily. I left for Ponte Vedra in the afternoon and got there in time for a beach house party across the street from Gail's. Completely staid until down I went to wander around a little bit, to find kids playing with all sorts of fun fireworks. The rowdier bunch, emboldened by beer, played something like laser tag, shooting roman candles at each other, then the loser had to line up and get shot at from, call it, 25 meters away. I did plenty of stupid stuff in my younger days, and my parents and grandfathers probably would have said what I'm about to, but I don't think that I would have done something that stupid. And yet there was a reckless abandon to it that made it look really fun. There was a buzz that made me wish I had.

July 5 / Jacksonville, FL

Alex returns to the trip tomorrow. I pushed everything back one day so he could spend one more day with his girlfriend. This holiday Monday became a really long morning, a really long afternoon.

And yet, before I knew it, Emily was at the beach house with Java.

She got there before I did. From a distance, I saw Java on the beach, letting me know she was there. Down I walked. A silhouette, she was talking to someone else. I thought she might have brought a friend or something, which had me pretty disappointed. But they kept walking and Em turned back toward me. She looked great, of course. A bit subdued. Java attacked me with yelps of joy and licks then went back to being attached to her at the hip.

I gave her a big hug and we walked around for a while, never really feeling as awkward as I thought it should feel.

There we were, together, or side by side at least, walking on the same beach where we had spent so much time in other circumstances. Evolved into where we had been before.

It was just nice to catch up, to hear her voice, to watch her listen to me talk about things I don't share with anyone else. And yet there was a finality to the get-together that hung over us. She planned to leave Java, go back to Brazil, and hopefully figure out for herself what she wanted to do with her life.

As I watched her go, she wished for me to do the same.

I kissed her by the cars. It felt comfortable and familiar only with no promises behind or in front. A kiss just to kiss her, to tell her I still love her, and always will.

Off she went to the latest vampire movie, Twilight I think, with her girlfriends in town, and there I held Java wishing to go back in time.

On Tue, Jul 6, 2010 at 10:04 AM
Emily <W▮▮▮▮▮▮▮▮▮▮▮▮▮▮▮▮▮▮▮>:

> Hey jase. > > I'm having a hard time today. Not sure if I'll make it to watch the game this afternoon. > > I'm feeling stressed about many things, like my life is in purgatory and I'm tired of feeling like this with no real answer to people when they ask me what I'm doing. I haven't accomplished anything since I've been home except for paying for one ticket only to get two more while driving in va.
> > That includes the lawyers. Two court dates have been moved. I need you to send in those two forms, signed. I don't know what we are doing or thinking, after all this time and pain. At this point, I would rather just get remarried if we find out later that it was all a big mistake. > > Sorry I'm just not doing so well with all these changes.

From: Jason McCarthy <▮▮▮▮▮▮▮▮▮▮▮▮▮▮▮▮▮>
Date: Tue, Jul 6, 2010 at 11:17 AM
Subject: Re:
To: Emily <▮▮▮▮▮▮▮▮▮▮▮▮▮▮▮▮▮▮▮>

ok, Em. will do. i'm sorry it's a tough day, i understand what you're feeling, as much as possible. lovejase

July 6 / Still in Jacksonville, FL

The hangover of a familiar and loving encounter put into a different context, the next day, made it harder to just view as one day in isolation. A tough morning, an offer to Emily to meet in St Augustine not well received. And then an invitation to her home with her mom to watch the World Cup game. So off we went, perhaps hard not to invite us, harder for us to even think about not going. We came in through the unlocked garage door. So much has changed, so much looks better about Alice's house and yet it has come at such a cost, for Emily to be there with nothing else to do but try to fix her mom's house, and the lives it represents.

The game was a nice reason to be there. We rooted for Uruguay as the underdogs but it was not meant to be. Despite some near heroics towards the end. It came time to say goodbye, but that time passed.

Em and I took Java for a walk after she cried a fair amount at my truck. And then I gave her the signed divorce papers, saying that wasn't supposed to be the final coda of the day, so we should head for the river with the pup.

We chatted and talked some more, the easy parts still infinitely easy, the hard parts lingering but not yet fully to the surface. We really love each other still, it's obvious.

I would like nothing more than to scoop her up and do the summer road trip with her, coast to coast, but we just can't. It broke my heart to tell her this, which she already knew. Maybe someday, but not just yet. We're still a ways off from that.

She has to go back and I have to go back, to somewhere not this moment on that driveway. Home to too many goodbyes already. And so I cried pulling out of it again this time, harder and different than all those that preceded it. Even more human than every weekend's hello goodbye when I was in the Army and she was teaching in Jacksonville. Even harder given the time we've cost ourselves in separation and in the love we have but can't share. And so I cried, half whole, and headed south to get back to the summer trek.

Versailles

July 7 / Miami

Little Havana is the coolest part of town, the influence is strong and integrated into its own neighborhood, its own way. Friendly and welcoming and entirely unapologetic. I was an outsider, but a welcomed one.

Versailles for lunch, plantain chips and a house special Cuban. Delicious, I took some to go to head to Domino Park with Java, who loved his portion of the sandwich as much as I loved mine. And so we laughed with the dominoes, and Java was adored by the players, and everyone was so friendly to us it made us want to come back again and again. Java and I walked around Calle Ocho. Alex met us and off we went to Key West.

We arrived just in time for the sunset, the tourists flocked to the best spot in town on the water to watch it go down. There is likely no place I've been that's more touristy, yet there's nothing that feels commercial about the sunset itself - left to your own perspective, it's the most private and pure experience, an imminently beautiful moment with nature, something that hasn't changed in this spot, something that won't change no matter what happens to the boardwalk, no matter how many key lime pie stands or artist exhibitions or t-shirt stalls there are. ==The sunset is worth it, every night.==

To the 90 miles to Cuba marker, couple pictures, and away we go to snag a hotel heading out of town. Loved Key West, didn't do the Hemingway house, this time. Have to save some things for next time.

> On Jul 7, 2010, at 12:17, Emily <██████████@gmail.com> wrote:
> >> Hey jase. I'm leaving on monday now, and returning in late august. Just wondering if you and Java and Alex are going to make a pit stop in jax on your way north. Love Em

> From: Jason J. McCarthy > To: ██████████@gmail.com > Subject: Re: Key west return > Sent: Jul 7, 2010 3:19 PM > > Ur tearing me up, Em. It's not ur fault, or mine, just the us part of it. I don't think I can stop through. Even as that makes me sad and cry in Little Havana right now, with Java panting under a tree but full off half my Cuban sandwich, you know, I'm sick of saying good bye to you, Em, with all of life up in the air. Just thinking about ur driveway has me crying. It was great to see you, you look great, and keep the faith. > Ok enuf heavy stuff, monster is doing well, he loves his road food, and some beach in the morning. But he didn't move in the back seat all morning. Tired from beach and pool etc. We r just hangin, waiting for Alex. Call whenevs. > Lovejaseandjav

On Wed, Jul 7, 2010 at 3:50 PM, Emily <██████████@gmail.com> wrote: > Hey jase. > > You are right, no more goodbyes. I can live with that, even if I'm hanging on a thread these days. Little Havana, that mutt gets to go everywhere. Lucky dog that he is. Sorry about germany, sucks to play for 3rd place now but at least some new teams get a chance at a world cup victory. I'll be in touch and thinking of you. And jav of course. Drive safely, always, and sell your stuff. Love you so xoxo Em

From: Jason McCarthy <██████████@gmail.com> Date: Wed, Jul 7, 2010 at 5:39 PM Subject: Re: Key west return To: Emily <██████████@gmail.com> Remember what I told you, Em. You're gonna be alright, you just need a little time. Take it easy on yourself, one day is not a universe, it's just one day. some better than others, but it's still just one day. have fun in brazil (call before you leave!) and be safe down there. oh yeah, and have fun. key west in an hour or so, i've been in kind of a foul mood today after leaving jax etc. life's tough sometimes, but we'll make it through. jav says mosterlick-monsterlick!!
xoxolove jase

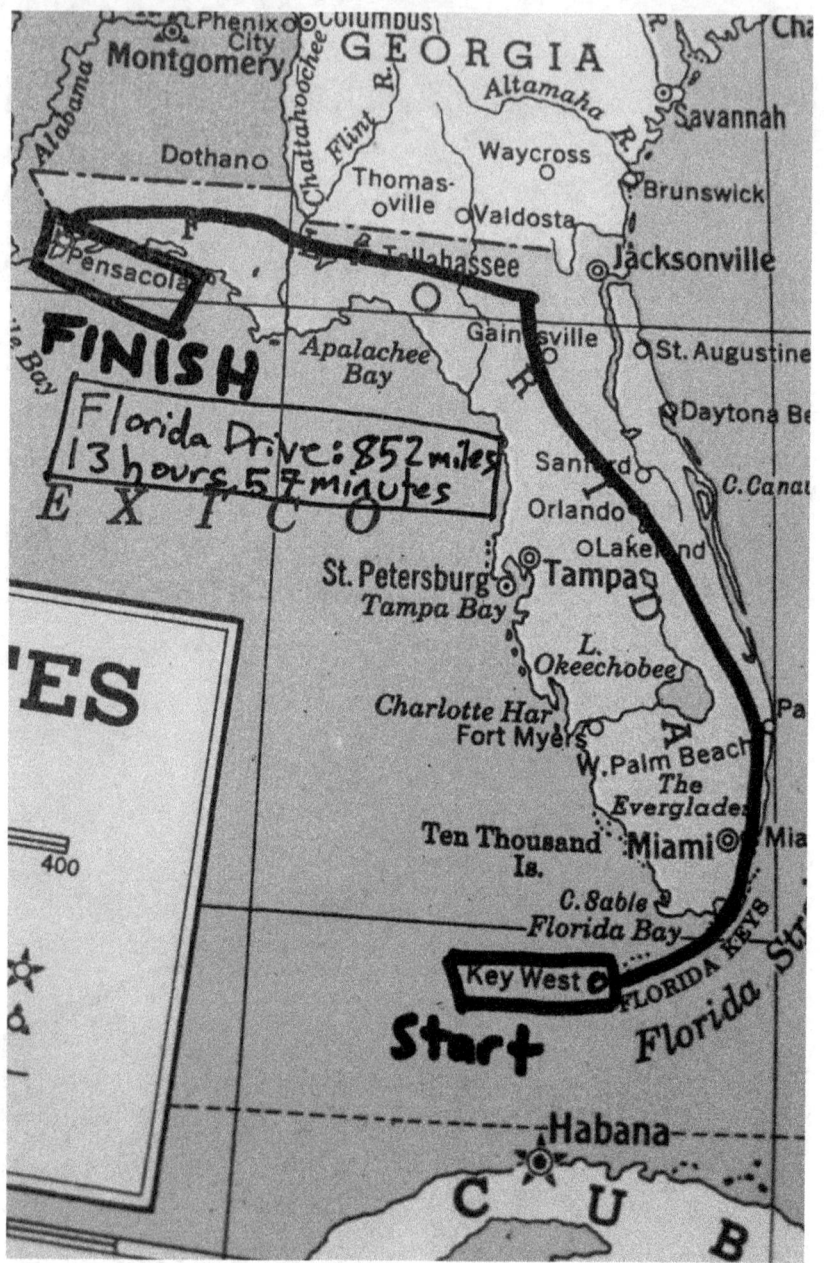

July 8 / Key West -> Pensacola

Started driving out of Key West last night, just a bit after hitting up Sloppy Joe's, which probably did not have as many pictures up of Hemingway when Hemingway was going there. Key West is so touristy but the sunset is so pristine, so beautiful, that no matter how many postcard stands there are, no matter how many magicians trying to sell a trick, the sunset is pure, and wonderful, and the reason why people go. And when all the faces are turned, it almost seems like they can't believe that they got such a bargain in the process, that it didn't cost anything. Except maybe a tip for a magician.

July 8 was driving day. Key West to Pensacola. Rolled in late to SAE, my brother Case's fraternity house. It was nice to see how my brother lives his life, even if just for a few hours of woken-up sleep. Java was welcomed, of course (it's a frat house), and I really enjoyed Case's friends, though I was almost in disbelief at the fact that they were in college. And young. I was long out and didn't want to be back in the frat house scene at all anymore. It's a shame and a Godsend to grow up. Pensacola, SAE

David Quesada
Pledge Educator

July 9 / Fairhope, Alabama

Left Pensacola and headed to Alabama, wanted to check out the Gulf area on the Alabama side before heading to New Orleans. Grabbed a coffee at Starbucks in Pensacola and asked what we should do in Mobile, which is when Fairhope was suggested as an alternative. So we went to Fairhope, especially because Alex and I had been to Mobile last summer and Fairhope would be something new. We headed for the water, the docks. Java sprinted ahead to the end and found several fisherman out and about, one who had pulled up 10 sharks already that morning and while we were standing there, another, which of course Java had to bark at and give a long inquiry.

We hung out on the docks a while, learning that this part of the Gulf was protected from the oil spill but that a lot had been blocked off, a lot of fishermen were unable to earn a living or had to move. But this fish was still good, and they recommended it, and ate it themselves.

We went into town and asked for "one spot" where the locals go for local fish, and that place was Wintzell's Oyster House. Java was happily included on the patio.

Sweet teas and catch of the day for us, with their award winning (in 3 states) seafood gumbo. I felt good spending money there, they say they need tourist dollars at a time when it's 75% down.

I was happy to be there, and to enjoy the fish, and recommend that others do the same.

July 9 / To New Orleans

I dropped Alex off at the Olivier House, our favorite hotel in town. Java and I walked around after that, until we met up with Jimmy, a local who we indirectly knew from Abidjan. He was the Regional Security Officer at the Embassy before I showed up. Java had met him, I had not.

Jimmy searched around forever for a parking spot before we met up for a beer, outside of course, with Java along for the ride. We hung out and drank the local stuff, chatted about this and that. Being a former Army guy in the State Department now, we have a lot in common. Great guy who has come back to New Orleans because it's home. He never expected to be back for good, but here he is and he wants to go nowhere else. I wonder if I'll ever settle in Jacksonville, or home, or what that all means.

What is home for me? I've been on the road, different places, for all of my life, the change is built into the home, and home is an ideal I don't really have. Or will one day Jacksonville be that place to me, as New Orleans is to Jimmy, that I never thought I would move back to, but then there I was?

Jimmy had to run, fighting a cold, so Java and I went to Coop's Place, a local bar just well known enough that tourists can find it, but no matter, everything was great. Java stole the show, as usual, and I enjoyed the time there, chatting up the bartender, who "Yes, I recommend the food" told me everything was good before telling me to get red beans with the fried chicken, so that's what we went with. Java and I both enjoyed it, and our walk around, before settling into the car for a nice long night of traffic and sirens and drunks yelling loudly to make sure you can hear them, just a couple blocks off Bourbon Street.

While I'm sick of doing everything on the cheap, we have no money, no revenue coming in, so the only way to make it is to cut costs.

And so we are cutting costs. I roll up the windows and sleep in the A/C.

How to pass Selection

From: Jason McCarthy <████████@gmail.com>
Date: Fri, Jul 9, 2010 at 2:35 PM
Subject: Re: Joining 20th Group REQUEST FOR ADVICE
To: Matthew ████████████████████████>

Matt, All this is coming from my recollection of a course I did in 2004, but I doubt it's changed much. (1) your feet. make sure they are calloused as fuck. I can't stress this enough. You don't want to be there fucking around with moleskin every night etc. You don't have the energy even though you do have the time. it sucks if your feet start falling off. To prep, get your feet wet at the beginning of a ruck -- train with 50 pounds (your rucks there have to be 45 lbs plus water and food, meaning 45 pounds when you get to the finish line) plus water. Train with thin socks. Thin thin thin and then upgrade when you go once you get the calluses your feet need. (2) land nav. Make sure you are comfortable with MGRS coordinates and a map with a compass. Learn about strategy of attacking the land nav (attack points, backstops etc). I recommend handrailing the roads (always more than 50 meters off though), covering more ground, and not getting lost in the shit that is thick next to the water. Walk around the messy shit. Trust me on this, walk more and fight through vines less. To do this strategy, you need to be very comfortable bearing weight on your back. At the end of the day, the more prep you put in, the more squared away you'll seem since you won't have to stress about shit like your feet. Having to fake being cool when you have huge blisters that kill you every step is not fun. As an officer, you better learn to smile and never ever complain. There will be some leadership stuff, I think, but I can't really tell you how to prep that. Basically, be well liked and you'll do fine. 'Play well with others' is something you'll hear often. The course itself is designed around day and night evals where you find points based off coordinates you get, and you receive your next points at the point you just found. There will be a guy in a tent or something like that who takes your roster number -- and assuming you're at the correct point (the course is not self-correcting), will give you your next grid. You have maybe 10 hours to get to 3 or four points. I can't remember exactly. Good luck, let me know if you have more questions.
--jason

That's a good dude right there.

July 10 / Habitat for Humanity / New Orleans, LA

We woke up, Java and I, bright and early with dripping windows from the condensation created by running the A/C all night. Cheaper than a hotel, it took me back to all the nights I would drive back and forth from Fort Bragg to see Emily. I would always stay with her as long as I could and arrive back to Bragg in the middle of the night, bedding down in my car next to wherever first formation would take place. But no regrets about that, other than that it should have been more normal. And here Java and I were, in New Orleans, sleeping in the car to save $100 we don't have.

So we woke up early and walked around, looking for some coffee. Even Café du Monde had a long wait for coffee, and the beignets weren't ready at the moment, so we got distracted by more walking and didn't make it back. And nothing else was open, so when we left the French Quarter at 7am for the worksite, the town was not yet itself, it was still coming to life with the people up much earlier than everyone else: runners, street cleaners, and restless tourists still up or waking up to not miss anything. The streets had an electricity to them, with a random 24 hour spot open, that promised another night of unique New Orleans fun.

Habitat for Humanity was a bit south of town, and we got there around 830 after grabbing breakfast and coffee en route. Dave, the project manager, was the type of guy who smiled all day about what he was doing and had the perspective to know that he was making a difference but that he couldn't stress out too much about the speed of the progress or he would drive himself crazy.

Some people aren't meant to do this kind of stuff, but they still want to, was his line I remember. Alex and I put in a day's worth of sweat into the houses, and learned a thing or two about what makes the program work, getting the buy-in from the people who also want Habitat to build them a house. We were happy and proud to be associated with this project, even if it was just for a day, and yes we felt like tourists, but the houses didn't care and the soon-to-be-owners were grateful for the help, so we got over it.

Back to Jimmy's place (no Java) to run in the rain a little bit to tire Java out and hang out, catch up on the Internet, and get a plan for the night. It was cool to see Jimmy's interior, with a lot of wood from Abidjan to take me back to the factory there, visiting Paul, and how sad that the government drove them out of business.

GRl & some attempt
to celebrate something

So we hung for a bit, took much needed showers, and went back to the Olivier house. Alex and I walked around, he half-heartedly took some pictures of me on the streets with GR1, and we settled into the patio at Lefitte's Blacksmith Shop bar for drinks outside. Loved the vibe there, the relaxed atmosphere of being off the Bourbon Street part of Bourbon Street, even a few blocks makes all the difference. We hung and smoked a few cigars from Miami, which were local there, and chatted up a few others who were starting their night as we were wrapping up ours. Back to the hotel, we passed out quickly.

July 11 / Cache drop at the Olivier House, love it there, a ton.

Taylor Grocery

July 11 / The Bulldog, in Jackson, MS en route to Oxford

The World Cup was on. I went inside to see about Java, he was a no-go, so I went outside to hang with him for a while before coming back in to grab a bite to eat. The bartender came over and told me he hated Java waiting in the car and that we should find a seat outside on the empty patio, so we did. Java had that relief to his panic step going, so he was thrilled to feel settled in next to me. We worked and watched Spain almost lose the World Cup, but ultimately take their first.

On the road to Oxford, we went first to Taylor Grocery in Taylor, MS. The wait was 30 minutes or so, and from my first step in the place I loved it. Loved it. Oxford is a preppy southern town with its traditions, and they are genuine and everyone takes pride in them. We love it. Live music, kids eating ice cream, singing along. The food is southern and homemade, that's tough to argue with, as authentic a place as you'll find. We met up with Lee's cousin Dave, who lives in a run-down house with a wall down in the middle so a duplex full of brothers became a full house, it was perfect for us.

That first night Alex and I went for a run over to Rowan Oak, Faulkner's old house, and checked out the square then settled back into a little small talk and catching up.

July 12 / Wildrose Kennels, Oxford

Blake greeted us around 9am and could not have been more friendly. He was ready for us, and gave us the full tour, talking a little bit softer than we like with not quite enough soundbites, but we made it work because he was so passionate and so knowledgeable about all that goes on there. Java hung in the car while we walked around and met everyone. It was a blast, being around the dogs, seeing how they're raised, and then letting Java swim around and get all the exercise he needed, and then some. I love this shop, the store, the grounds, and hope we are able to sell through them. With no real reason to leave town, we decided to work on our, ummm, work, and stay another night before leaving for Nashville.

After running Java around to Rowan Oak, Faulker's House, again, we went to Ajax Diner in town, I had the catfish salad to have something local with at least a little green. Food on the road can be quite brown by default, so it's nice to get a little green in there from time to time. Friendly people there. We bounced around for a couple drinks and a few laughs, settling into a bar with a Brooklyn band playing bluegrass in Oxford, and trying really hard to be authentic. Too authentic, but the music was great and they were super talented, so we had a great time and settled back into a nice night's sleep.

From: Jason McCarthy <█████████████████>
Date: Mon, Jul 12, 2010 at 6:45 PM
Subject: GORUCK Introduction
To: <█████████████> // GR MAILING LIST

Friends and family, As you know, I started GORUCK (www.GORUCK.com) in 2008 as I was completing my time in the Special Forces. GORUCK was born of the idea to take the best from the military backpacks and gear I had used all over the world while streamlining the look and feel to be simpler and more urban. We retained the durability, functionality, and ability to customize, and ensured superior quality by hand building all GORUCK gear in the United States at a time when nearly everyone else is offshore. Yes, you pay more, but you get what you pay for. We use military-grade materials and construction and all of our rucksacks come with a Lifetime Guarantee.

On May 1, 2010 GORUCK officially launched at Tough Mudder, an adventure race started by British Special Forces and billed as the 'toughest one day endurance race on the planet.' We put together a team of current and former Green Berets and ran the race with our rucksacks filled with bricks to prove that GORUCK bags can withstand anything. Check out the full story at our GORUCK summer blog: www.gorucksummer.com GORUCK backpacks are simply the toughest backpacks on the planet, suitable for all adventures and sleek enough for any urban environment (our latest write-up in Details magazine). www.details.com/blogs/daily-details/2010/07/back-in-black.html. But GORUCK is meant to be so much more than just a gear company; GORUCK is an American brand, inspired by my time as a Green Beret, the United States of America and its open roads, and a reverence for people who take pride in their daily lives.

GORUCK has hit the open roads this summer to meet people, get into adventures, and share the story as it happens. We're driving through all 48 continental states ending with our nation's capital in late August. The lead character in our adventure is the United States, with summer as an epic stage (is there anything more American than the summer?)

The best part of the trip so far has definitely been the people we've met and the stories we've heard, in the big cities and off the beaten path. We're overwhelmed by the good we find everywhere we go: East Coast to West Coast, the South, the Midwest, everywhere, nationwide.

Please follow us at www.goruck.com/news forever and this summer at www.gorucksummer.com for a full slice of adventure and Americana, GORUCK style. Also, please 'like' us at www.facebook.com/GORUCK. Thanks so much for your continued support. As GORUCK is a grassroots brand, please support us by forwarding this to your friends and contacting me with any opportunities I should not miss.

Best, Jason McCarthy Founder, GORUCK

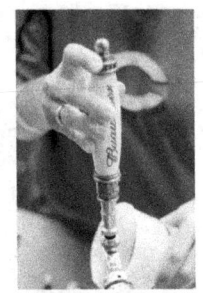

Cold beers in a hot summer

COLONEL THEODORE ROOSEVELT

July 13 / Oxford -> Nashville, TN

To Nashville late in the afternoon so we could take it easy. Went to breakfast with our host and hostess before seeing them off to work and chilling in the house most of the day. Chatted with Alex about the 'branding' we needed moving forward, he was really supportive and we moved to get Jack with us sooner than later to that effect. Drove to Nashville, got in kinda late and nestled up in the Borders. I uploaded the Details Magazine article and Alex worked.

I dropped him off a Riccha's place and went to find a cheap motel with Java, where we could settle in for the night. It was late and we were hungry so we grabbed some Waffle House to go and went back to the room to drink a few beers, eat an egg or three, and pass out.

July 14 / Nashville -> Franklin TN

Late check out, headed to Abernathy Road to talk to Brett. Really liked the store, thought Brett had something special there and that his style made it work. I related my story of time in Nashville and our GORUCK story for a while, he told me how big the Details magazine spot was and his plans for the store, that people either get it or they don't. It's a Colonel Littleton outpost, and the more I saw of the work, the more I wanted to head down to see him. I gave Brett some dead silence after I told him I wanted to be in Nashville because of its uniqueness, because of my background, because of where we were going with things, and I watched his wheels turning. The word consignment came up, but since the stores are more a branding tool than anything else, it didn't really bother me from him. He's gotta make his store run, I get it, and he's a great ambassador for GORUCK, and he lets us move our philosophy forward of why we sell to certain stores. The more we can get to tie us in with American quality, the better.

I had Alex come in and take pictures of the place so that we could better brand our story of why we wanted to be sold in there. Then I headed over to Imogene and Willie's, talked to their manager for a long while about his shop, and my line, before showing him the product. Price point's tough, he said. It's an awesome shop along South 12th, the type of shop I imagine for GORUCK, with seamstresses on site and a really cool vibe in there. Small product offering but everything customizable, hand built to your specs. Java and I went to the creek and avoided a $175 ignorance ticket we were told he'd get for being off the leash. Wore him out, snagged Alex, who was not in the best of moods, and we headed to Franklin to stay in the sticks with Chris, my old neighbor, after grabbing a burger and a beer at Battleground Ale, which was inauthentically authentic.

Outside Nashville

The dog park on the old Civil War battleground was great, though, en route to the burbs to get to Chris's house.

I love all these places you take me to, Alex said, half-joking and the other, more serious side knowing that he actually was.

For all the time and energy spent getting free beds, it was worth it to add to the real experience.

Chatted with Chris about solitude, OK not directly, but about living in the sticks and how much he loved it, and how he spends his hard time away from home. But he loves it, content to his quiet space.

Alex slept with one of Chris's many guns by his head, and felt all the more awkward for it, and we woke up early to head to Colonel Littleton's.

"The Colonel"

July 15 / Lynnville, TN / Colonel Littleton, Maker's Mark

830 arrival in Lynnville coming from Chris's house. Java got a nice walk on fog-covered back roads and rolling Tennessee hills before an hour-long drive. We got there, the staff was super friendly and the Colonel wasn't there yet. I grabbed a $1 coffee next door and walked around. As we started to meet everyone, it was clear that Java was very welcomed all around the grounds. We started the tour, I didn't know what to make of the Colonel exactly. A really great man that everyone respected, I didn't get him until he asked me, while Alex was getting his equipment out of the car, what we were doing here. I told him the story about how we wanted to associate with quality and America and to be a real icon, like he was. He remembered our names for the entire day, used them repeatedly, and worked in every talking point I mentioned about his own store in such a way that lets us speak to GORUCK at the end of it. A real pro, who seemed to really care and want me to succeed, he welcomed us in as family and spared no time or effort or energy to tell us how his shop is run, and run well, and why he has been successful. ==I learned more this morning than I did in an entire year of business school.==

We left around noon after making a lot of new friends there, and sped to Maker's Mark for a tour. The grounds were beautiful, we picked the perfect spot to do our feature. Another icon, founder of the Bourbon Trail, and committed to a slower, more quality conscious way of doing things. The water, the lake we saw, was the special part of the trip for me, for us. It's real, the 'materials' are real, and even though it becomes iconic later on, this is the foundation.

We powered through to Mt Adams, Cincinnati, met up with Alex's friend's brother Blake, had a beer and a burger. I planted a Cache and did a quick walk around with Java. We drank a UDF milkshake while he ate a few hotdogs from there, and life was good. To Bellbrook late, we had a few beers with my dad in the garage and called it a night.

July 16 / Bellbrook, OH / Friday

First full day in Bellbrook. Ran around the soybean field with Java, hung out and worked, Alex had a ton of editing to do. So we waited around for the grill out, people trickled in around 5 or 6 and it was on.

All the familiar faces, some out of place, like seeing my mom and dad together, with all of my dad's friends, at my dad's house. And yet I love being here for the intersection of people from different places and different times in my life. So I walked around, everyone asking about GORUCK, and I talked and talked about it to their heart's delight. ==The beautiful thing is that everyone has so many ideas for it, the hard thing is that everyone has so many good ideas for it, the focus is challenging.== Jack couldn't make it here for the party, Uncle John made him stay the night in Sundance with Ashe to make sure they'd be alright. He left Saturday morning. Cornhole Friday night was a blast. Alex and I lost to some locals, but only barely, so I almost didn't feel bad about it.

Dick and Donnie, love those guys, known them forever, it's nice when some things in life don't change as I change so constantly. Up late and later, till 230 or so, drinking in the garage, which is what you do in Bellbrook at my dad's place. Dad and Les worked too hard to put it all on, Les especially stresses about it, but everyone had a great time, Leila as well, who Les tells me felt like she had a family on this night, with me around, with something she could associate with that she believed in. A good night's sleep followed.

My dad at Sturgis —
Mount Rushmore

July 17 / Bellbrook, OH / Saturday

Casual morning of a run with Java, work on the computer, and a plan to get Jack at 3. Until we realized, most of the way there, that Jack wasn't getting in until 630, so Alex and I diverted to the Air Force Museum, killed a couple hours ('wicked museum' he called it), and snagged Jack. The museum took me straight back to all the times I went there with my grandfather, 'Big', the movies we'd watch, the slight boredom at going but the excitement of doing it with him, even then to see him excited made me equally as excited, and those memories are worth their weight in gold now. Every time I go back there it's as if my grandfather is there with me.

Jack's arrival was greeted with all smiles other than the flight time mix-up. It was good to see him, talking a mile a minute about everything and excited to be here with us. We got home and brainstormed a long while about what we wanted to accomplish.

The picture of my dad at Sturgis turned the tide for us. Alex said that picture was so GORUCK we should just own it. The stamp-it metaphor was born, and it made sense of the entire summer at that point, where the pictures we have taken can be used for branding purposes and to simply stamp with GORUCK. We place them next to a product shot, or not even, and we have a brand being built. Blue Angels, stamp it. Etc.

Leslie said it was fun to listen to us think about all of this stuff together, to see how we worked it out in our heads. And it was fun for me, for us, as we felt so privy to a conversation, in my dad's kitchen, that was furthering our company in large strides, before we could even action it. We knew the power of what we were saying, everyone felt energized to come back and get to work.

I got my list to Alex and everyone was excited. Around us at the house, it turned into the night before, of course. We were up for cornhole and everything, plus some random friends of Terry's showed up to hang out as well. Pete among them. We played cornhole back and forth, the competition between Alex and Java for the worst cornhole player settled on Alex as the worst.

We were up top doing our thing when Terry came up and said there had been an accident, that a couple quad runners were in the river, and that Pete was 'pretty fucked up'.

So down we went, I got asked immediately if I knew what to do in something like this. Just having been through a crash myself, and knowing the shock involved, all Pete needed was for someone to take charge and tell him it was going to be OK.

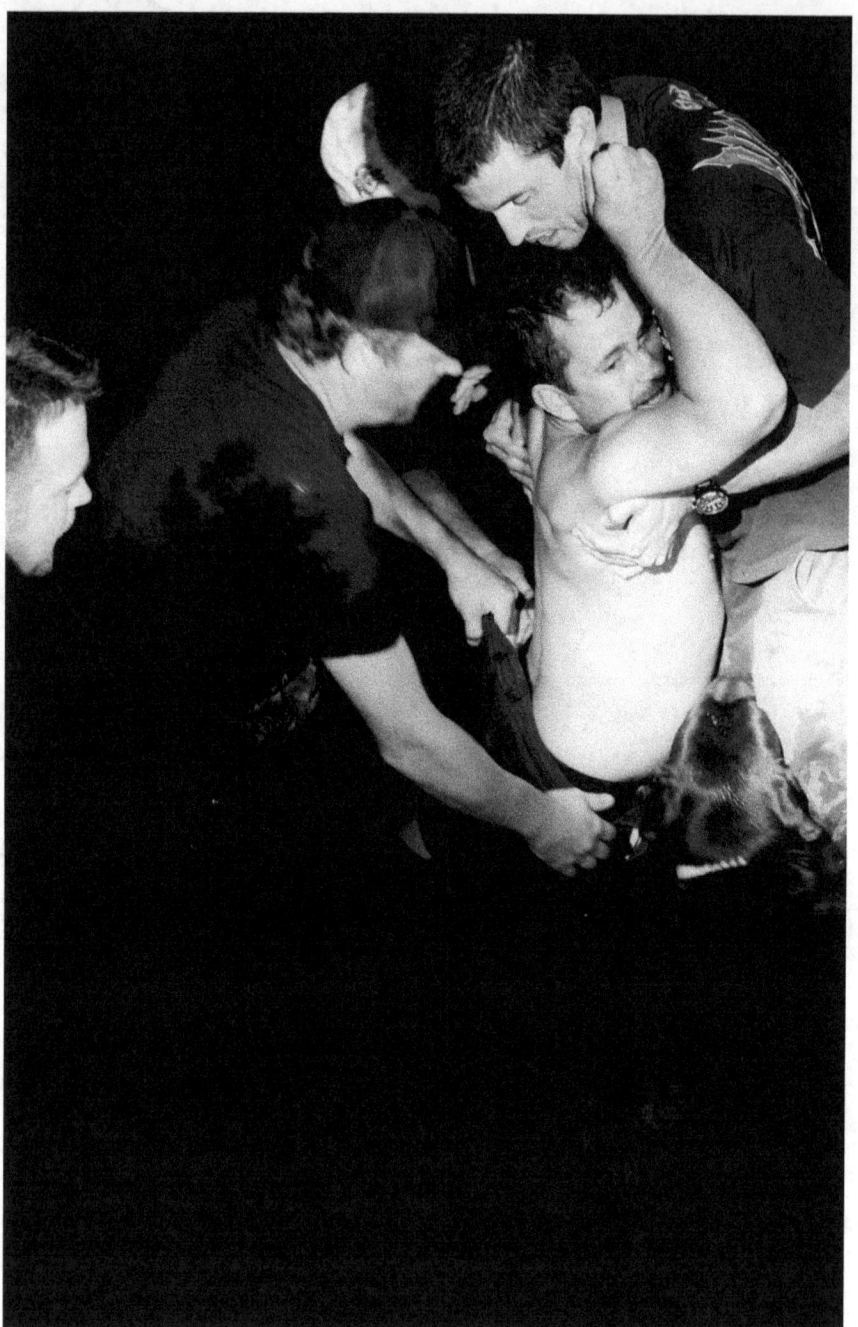

So we pulled him out of the river, one slippery and slow step at a time, and got him to the bank, and onto the quad runner, and up top. The ambulance answered the call, I told them there was some shock but nothing life threatening.

Of course they sent the entire department, I guess bored no doubt. Turns out Pete got charged with a DUI, which he can fight if he wants to. I have no idea exactly what went on, I'm just glad that everything turned out OK, and I'm sure Pete is all the wiser for the night because of that.

In case you enjoy running through soybean fields, we have a ruck for you.

The Blue Angels

Sunday July 18 / Bellbrook, OH

The morning bled over from the night before, so there was a late wake-up. We headed to the Air Show around 130 or so, and spent the next 3 hours just taking it in. Alex and I were there for shots, Jack and my dad mostly to hang out and enjoy the ride. It was different than I remember it from my youth, different but somehow a little better. The overcast skies cooled it down, made it less scorching hot, even the brief showers were welcomed. I don't remember as much asphalt. I remember picnics with jello squares, a blanket on a grassy field, and a scorching sun. This go round we took it all in, eagerly awaiting the Blue Angels to come out, and were not disappointed when they finally did. The speed, the people, the quality of the show, all great.

To Palmer's house to get some shots on his old Harley. Jack and Alex messed around with it a little bit, Alex grumpy with lack of food or whatever else. The shots looked weird, bike is too small, but the shots of the manbarn were awesome, and Palmer's set up is a solid one, worthy ground for many a legendary night.

Back to the house, same old same old. Up drinking, working, chatting.

No reception in the garage. No emails coming in anyway.

July 19 / Dayton, OH

Turned into a day at the house, working and editing, editing and working. Pictures on the grounds full of poison ivy. At night we went out to the Oregon District to get some urban shots to complement the green shots Alex and Jack got that day, and the motorcycle shots we got in the driveway. It was kind of cool to see Alex and Jack work together, Alex at the helm, another side of it felt really contrived in a way I don't envision GORUCK being at all. But that's the nature of it, the pictures that we need. Or do we, should I be more challenging the assumption that we need model-style still shots for our campaign. Action energy and purpose should always be at the front of it, emanating through the pictures. Are we telling the story well enough? Not yet, sales are non-existent and I'm not happy with the website, with the way things are going overall. It's too conservative, not telling the story enough, not challenging the simplicity we're going for but we are not yet leveraging what we have to the best of our ability. Back to the casa for more nighttime festivities centered around the computer until my dad comes home around 1130, then a few hours up with him before bed.

July 20 / Caesar Creek, OH / Tuesday

Boating with Phil in the morning, we got our water skiing shots we wanted. Phil took off work like a champ to help us out. Caesar Creek, where I used to go as a kid, was the destination. More like a lake than a creek, it was great to feel the wind, and the sun, for a day when, if we were playing by the rules, we'd be in an office doing silly stuff somewhere else. Phil took a couple runs before Jack went out. Jack was out there too long, stupidly, because he has no idea when to stop. Or to say no. So on he went, fall after fall, trying to get up on one ski. Alex stole a picture or two that makes it look like he did, but eventually we had to cut him off. I did a couple, Alex did a couple, then my dad. I remember not being able to stand up last time I did this, in the middle of Osgood-Schlatter's where my knees constantly ached in college, so I was thrilled to be able to get up and enjoy it. I love the adrenaline but I'm cautious about some things, water skiing is one of them. The older I get, the less I want to feel stupid pain, pain brought on that I know I can avoid. So I enjoyed being pulled, didn't do anything too crazy, and when after my 4th time up I slammed my knee into the ski, that was all she wrote for me.

The boys mostly hung out and got some other shots today, I have grown reclusive trying to get some revenue into GORUCK, which makes for long days making calls and presentations.

Talked to Michael at A Continuous Lean, love that guy and am excited for him to cover us a little bit. He's totally into us. Yelled at Jack after him telling me how hard he was working on everything, after me telling him for the second week to get me a priorities list better than the half-assed one he sent me before, saying that tomorrow I may have to fucking beg. There are issues with Jack and his organization, or lack thereof, that are troubling me. Wildrose saw him as a freak when he calls what he did there 'holding court'. Not a good look. But Brett at Abernathy Road liked him, the biggest issue is that he has sold 5 bags so far this summer, which means he isn't even covering his per diem. And he can hold it over me all he wants that I screamed at him in NYC, but he got hammered, picked a fight with me about money, and then told me he was going to fucking knock me the fuck out. So he bit off more than he could chew. But I was the yeller, he's right, and he can get my temper, one of the few, because I love him and I care.

Dinner with Leslie and Leila at El Toro, good meal in a strip mall, but good to see Les and Leila out and about.

July 21 / Bellbrook, OH / Wednesday

My worst day of poison ivy yet, it just wasn't getting any better, and the shower I took to help was the least comfortable episode with this silly ailment I've had yet, despite getting it at Camp Mackall every time we went into the field. So I got out and went to the clinic, got my medicine, and I've been doing better since. Called it an earlier night with fewer beers than usual, and woke up on Thursday feeling somewhat better about life in general, I was not super fly TNT or the guns of the navarone as I was the night before.

Talked to Les at the house a while, her telling me we had never connected but that she loved me and wasn't going anywhere, nor was I, and that we should be closer. So I listened and shared a little bit, telling her I thought she was great but that it's hard to connect with me right now.

And it is, I have a lot of guards up at this stage in my life, more than I have been brought up to have.

But I'm glad she hit me up, even as I was stressed about missing out on getting some work done. I'm not sure what will change. I think that it's better to have the cards on the table and see where the hands go from there. Lead with transparency.

July 22 / Bellbrook, OH / Thursday

Feeling better, I hung out at the place, not running or exercising still, though, and got some presentations out into the world of businesses bigger and more successful than mine. Went to dinner with Nana at Mamma Disalvo's, had a lovely waitress, Stephanie. If things were different, I would have asked her out in a heartbeat. But I was content to get my pictures, have a story to tell, and then head home to my dad's.

I laid it out for Jack on the back porch, told him his updated list was better but that he needed to bring in some revenue. Period. That he needed to ask people for money, to support what he believes is a superior product.

He mostly listened and then disappeared to bed early, not all smiles for once. I retreated to the computer, antisocial as usual, under the pressure of a great company with no revenue, and on the line for everything.

My dad got home around 1130pm, I said hey and went back to typing. Until I realized that life is short and the days I have left in this world with my dad are numbered. So I headed out and we drank a couple beers in the garage, and then in the kitchen, and we joked and smiled about life and his friends, and mine. And Java.

And I slept all the better for it.

This is us, trying to figure out product photos, trying to make our gear look real.

We had a ways to go.

Popeye

July 23 / Bellbrook, OH / Friday

I filled our first anonymous order online, headed to Japan. The same guy I back and forthed with after I sold him a hat. It felt good, I guess, but anticlimactic as it was too long overdue. I don't love the thrill of selling, of fulfilling orders, of such a 'monumental' moment, our first Internet sale. We are global before domestic, story of the day with the Internet.

Back to the place to hang out and let my poison ivy sit in the A/C. While I can imagine how much worse off I would be were I not in America, with drugs and A/C, I'm glad I didn't have to. Any sweat whatsoever was immediate discomfort, so I remained inside to grit my teeth.

Kayaking with Terry's kayak. Pete's kayak, rather. Pete is still in the hospital, getting better, but still in a bad place to be in. DUI, broken bones, and shame. Of an accident and of breaking an ATV on your home turf with no good reason.

Palmer and Popeye stopped by to drink a few beers. A few led to a few more, I love hanging out with those guys.

Mini-golf, beer, back for cornhole, listening to songs on the computer till my dad came home with Leslie.

Up late, as usual.

Back on the road tomorrow.

NOTICE OF CITATION
CITY OF BOULDER PHOTO ENFORCEMENT PROGRAM
For detailed Photo Enforcement information, please visit
http://www.bouldercolorado.gov/court

The city of Boulder initiated the photo enforcement program, as allowed by state law, in an effort to increase safety, reduce accidents, and increase compliance with traffic laws. **The purpose of this letter is to inform you that your vehicle was photographed by the photo enforcement system, and that the driver pictured has violated a city of Boulder traffic ordinance.** If you are not the driver pictured, we ask for your support in making the streets safer by designating the driver of your vehicle in the space provided on the back side of the Notice of Citation.

Boulder Municipal Court
Violations Bureau
1777 6th Street (P.O. Box 8015)
Boulder, Colorado 80306-8015
(303) 441-1810

MC JASON JEROME

PONTE VEDRA BEACH, FL 32082

VEHICLE DESCRIPTION
Year	Make	Model	License	State
2000	NISS	UT	773WFV	FL

VIOLATION INFORMATION

Location of Offense	Arapahoe @ 30th St E/B		
Date Of Offense 06/24/2010	Time Of Offense 10:10:53 AM	BRC Section Number 7-4-3	
Complaint Officer		Badge Number	
Nature of Offense	OBEDIENCE TO RED SIGNAL REQUIRED		
Mail Date 07/06/2010		Letter Number	

The fine for this violation is **$75**. You, or the driver you nominate, may pay this amount on or before the response date of **07/21/2010** and close this case.

After this date, the Boulder Police Department will review this violation and issue a Summons and Complaint. This begins the personal service process, which carries an additional fee of $60.00. Delinquent cases are referred to a collection agency. This impacts your credit rating and increases the total amount due by 25%. This violation will not be a part of the operator's driving record, and **no points will be assessed**.

If you wish to contest this violation, you must contact the Boulder Municipal Court Violations Bureau on or before the response date noted above. Please have this document and your driver's license available.

See reverse side for additional information.

PAYMENT STUB   Plate    Letter No.:

If you elect to pay your fine, the amount due (listed above) must be paid in full by the response date specified. Payment closes this matter.
1. **To pay by internet using Visa or Mastercard**, visit www.bouldercolorado.gov/court and click the links for photo enforcement and then Pay-by-Web. **Your PIN NO. is**
2. To pay by mail:
   - Check, money order, or cashier's check must be made payable to the "City of Boulder". **DO NOT SEND CASH**
   - To make a credit card payment, please fill out the credit card information on the right portion of this stub.
   - Return this payment stub with your **full payment** in the envelope provided. Mail by the response date noted above.

This penalty shall not be a part of your driving record. **No points will be assessed** against your driving record as part of this traffic violation, except for violations exceeding the posted speed limit by 25 mph or more.

Court Questions – Call (303) 441-1810

Credit Card Payment by Mail
___VISA ___MC (16 DIGITS)

EXP DATE

Phone Number (___) ___

CARDHOLDER'S NAME

CARDHOLDER'S SIGNATURE

$_____
Total Fine Amount
Partial Payments Not Accepted

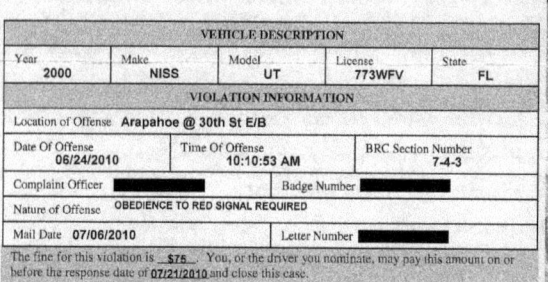

"Obedience to Red Signal Required"

Boulder, Colorado / Three Weeks Ago

They mailed my mom a letter, she scanned it and sent me a note, "happy to pay if you need me to."

Jack ran a red light in Boulder, $75 and they got pictures from every angle.

Our first ticket of the summer. It's really just insult to injury at this point. Not selling anything, racking up costs. We've been really good at talking our way out of tickets, the electronic cameras are a little harder to reason with, though, so I mailed the check in and tried to forget about it.

It feels like Big Brother is watching, can't we just do this the old fashioned cat and mouse way? If they want to give everyone a ticket for everything why don't they just put cameras everywhere?

July 24 / Akron, OH / Saturday / Soap Box Derby

En route to Akron, parking now for the Soap Box. So we showed up having already paid for 3 tickets, but apparently we were too late to get our tickets, so we just got stubs we didn't need. I asked about Java, if he could come in, and I was told that there were a lot of dogs around and could bring him. So out we went, and he started stealing the show, as usual.

I went up the hill a bit, distancing myself from Jack and Alex, and took Java up with me. We chatted up a few people before Jav and I skirted under the yellow tape, up to the top where the boxcars stage and start the race.

The vibe was so laid back as to be questionably good, and I'm not the pessimistic type. No 'pros' there, it felt like we were at an event minus all, or at least most, of the drama that consumes the big ones. **It felt more like a state fair, with the optimism of a youth's summer, than an NFL game consumed by concession sales and luxury boxes.**

And yet we learned of the financial difficulties at the Derby and hope that changes, sooner than later, but if it doesn't it would probably just stay local, and the locals would enjoy it just as much, with the locals to the sport working just as hard and hoping for the best, without the big bucks around to spoil the time.

Java and I meandered on up to where the press was, the announcers and the start line itself. Everyone loved Java, he stole the show, and they all wanted to pet him, and give him water, and hold on to him while I moved around with my camera.

Alex followed suit and made it up there, too, after a while, and was everywhere, until it was time to go, and the winner was declared, and we left smiling with a near empty track around us, wondering why this event wasn't covered to a much larger extent.

Though I've never seen it on TV, I suspect some of the innocence is lost on the viewer as it streams through the same set, with the same filter, as all the other sporting events.

On to Cleveland, ran into Grealis (a buddy from business school) on the street. He happened to be going to the store after not answering my texts.

He looked a bit rough around the edges, saying he got pretty lit up the night before.

A rooftop in Cleveland

Grabbed a burger at the Cleveland Ale House with Jack and Java and Alex before meeting up with Tyler at the liquor store. We headed up to the rooftop to drink our beer and watch the sunset.

I'm a bit distanced and removed from the daily life of the road these days, instead really opting for time with Java and time to work on getting some revenue into GORUCK.

Jack is disappointing me in his lack of initiative and unwillingness to ask for business. So it's more time I have to spend on him, and on doing it myself. With Java I mean, of course, my main sanity check.

So Jack drank the most, and stayed out the latest, and is still sleeping at 11am on Sunday.

July 25 / Cleveland, Ohio

Wake-up at Paul's place, slept on the floor next to Java, great location, sort of, though the scene is a little rough around here at night. Certainly not that chill. Lots of bass in the neighborhood. Went for a wet walk with Java, in the rain, to grab some coffee. And then back to the computer, to upload the blog post for Akron and shamelessly promote our stuff.

Jack worked on his sales plan. Unfortunately it just wasn't working. His plan or mine, or ours. He made a long list, I replied back:

Revenue.

I want daily updates on people you're asking for sales from. Not just stores, but friends. Revenue. Give friends half off, I don't care, cut deals, but we are failing to bring in enough. We aren't covering your per diem. Let alone costs. So I've started dedicating a lot more time to selling to any friend I've ever had. We have to figure out a way to get some support out of friends, any fucking body, don't care, but focus on revenue daily. Consignment is fine, get our inventory out there to stores we want to be in.

Priorities

1 - Revenue revenue revenue. We are not doing well with this. At all. Minimize costs and ask everyone for money to buy bags. If you can't tell, I'm getting hammered on this. So don't make me beg you to beg people. Anyone with two nickels to rub together is a target.

2 - Stores. Subset of #1, need presence stuff, too.

3 - Press. This is a larger beast but requires a lot of contact as well, lots of nets. Photographers, anyone who used to love you. Etc. Yes, etc.

4 - Keep engaging people for the long haul. Doing well at this. But this is last on the list because it's the easiest.

July 26 / Cedar Point, OH

World's fastest roller coasters. Got a contact info online, sent a note. Heard back, got free passes to the park.

> Hello Robin, My name is Jason McCarthy and I'm the founder of a company called GORUCK (www.GORUCK.com). I was in the Special Forces (Green Berets) for 5 years and started a military inspired line of retail bags and gear. But our branding is such that we are associating ourselves, as a brand, with the USA (all GORUCK gear is made in America), the summer (is there anything more American than summer?) and all of the best companies we like, nationwide. We have so far visited 40 states and done several videos/profiles on people and places. Our full summer blog is www.gorucksummer.com. Other places we have featured include Maker's Mark Bourbon in Kentucky, Wildrose Kennels in Oxford, MS, Beck Boots in Amarillo, TX, Agassi's school in Las Vegas, Colonel Littleton in Tennessee, Oklahoma Joe's BBQ in Kansas City, and many more. The common thread is that these places are iconic and uniquely American in their own right. I am an Ohio native of Dayton, I've been coming to Cedar Point since I was a boy, and I believe it represents the best of a summer experience at an amusement park. I would love to come late next week and do a feature on the park and our experience at it. You will notice that all of our blogs are meant to be overwhelmingly positive and portray the best that a place has to offer. I would really love to discuss this with you. Sincerely, Jason McCarthy Founder, GORUCK

After a few more back and forths, Robin eventually agreed. We stopped by the office, the lady told us to wait a minute. Robin showed up with our tickets, and talked to us about the history of the park. Robin walked us through the turnstiles, his badge worked just like our tickets did. He joined us for our first ride which meant we got to skip the line, and ride it with him. The rest of the day was not so fast. The lines were long, and great for thinking about all the stuff that wasn't going our way. We needed cash, it felt like we're just burning money every single day. Nobody is buying anything. Jack told me I should try to have more fun. I told him he should try to sell more rucks. Something, anything. He got mad, I got mad, Alex took pictures of roller coasters.

I went to the car in the parking lot and pulled out my laptop and went back to the 'everyone I've ever known in my life' list. I started calling them, one by one. This lasted for hours. I sold nine rucks, all at half off. Made something like $1,200. A fortune. The guys came back to the car hours later, asking me what I had been doing. Said I had to call people all afternoon to get them to buy rucks, we're running out of money. I looked at Jack and said he needed to do the same thing - make a list and call everyone on the list, I still had a lot of people to go through. This can't go on like this forever. He looked down and then said he couldn't just call everyone he knew and tell them to buy a bag, he had to do it his way. I shook my head and thought what the fuck are we even doing. We hit the road, then rolled into a campsite late, after hours. No bonfire, no beer, nothing. We didn't even

Park & Sleep wherever

really need a campsite, just a place with some ground to put our sleeping bags down. Alex and Jack put their sleeping bags down, I went to walk around with Java.

The moon was as bright as the brightest nights at Camp Mackall, those nights that feel like they're daytime. When there's no moon or it's completely cloud-covered, everything is harder, the stresses worse. Am I in the right place? I thought it was here. This night was an easy night for walking around. A few folks were still awake, I waved as I walked by, they waved back.

When Java and I got back, I put some OFF! on my face and the opening of my sleeping bag. Green Beret cologne, we call it. Java crawled in the bag with me, and eventually I fell asleep.

I woke up early, before the guys. Took Java for another walk. Came back, Alex and Jack both had mosquito bites all over their faces. Told me this place sucks. 'Look at my fucking face!' Alex said. I almost laughed and told him he was a dumbass for not using the OFF! Instead, I said nothing at all, something I was increasingly fine with. I said alright, let's go.

July 27 / Put-In-Bay, Ohio

Jack and I, screaming in the parking lot with all the tourists around. Alex just listening. They went on the boat to the island, I took Java to Sunset Park, lakefront gravel beach perfect to think about my life.

This is horrible.

I picked the guys up at the end of the day, Jack said he didn't expense anything. I had a friend of a friend's place to sleep at outside Detroit.

I drove, The National's High Violet - Bloodbuzz Ohio did all the talking. Nobody said anything. I still owe money to the money to the money I owe The floors are falling out from everybody I know I'm on a bloodbuzz Yes I am I'm on a blood, buzz

How to sleep for free all over America.

July 28 / Ann Arbor, Michigan

Kurt Cobain said one time that the Blind Pig in Ann Arbor was his favorite place to play, ever. That's cool, let's check it out. Completely dead, not even open. Bars on the windows. We walked around a little more and went and sat outside on some street by the campus of that team up north. We ordered some beers.

Jack said it was time for him to go home, I felt relieved like that scene in the Big Lebowski, a load has been lifted. Alex sat there looking angry but didn't say anything.

When Jack went to the bathroom I asked Alex if he was gonna quit, too. He said he was in through the Chicago race, as planned.

Nobody wanted to go to the Blind Pig or do anything really, and of course Java couldn't come in so there was really no good reason to go in, and away we went.

Jack got a flight out of Detroit for the next day. We crashed at some creeper's house, a friend of a different guy from business school, in the Detroit suburbs. He told us matter of fact this was the only night we could stay there. He didn't drink beer and said he had an early morning so he went to bed.

Jack and I walked around the block a few times. Told each other I love you man. This has been really hard.

Suburban Detroit was the backdrop. grass that hasn't been cut in too long, weeds and dying bushes. Round and round the neighborhood we went. By the end we picked up a couple pizzas from Little Caesars and a case of beer and wound down the night in the creeper's basement, where I barricaded the door shut.

July 29 / Suburbia, Detroit

We got kicked out of the house in the morning, thank you very much. Went to the Holiday Inn Express to use their Internet, which never had a password. Then some sports bar while we waited around for Jack's flight. I had every order from our website set up to deliver an email to my phone. It didn't go off, ever, so it wasn't part of my life. While we were sitting there, at the same time, we got two emails back to back. One guy had bought a full price GR2, that's $395, and we heard back from this fashion store in Soho called Odin that they wanted to carry our rucks.

Jack showed me the Odin email, I showed him the $395 order.

It was the first time we had smiled about work stuff in a long time. Jack went to the bathroom and cried, said he was so overcome by emotion.

We dropped him off at the airport on a high. Hey follow up with Odin when you get to town, first thing. Yeah yeah, of course, he said. This is what I need to be doing now. I nodded. I love you man. I love you too. And off he went. And then there were three.

Me, Alex, and Java.

July 30 / Harbor Springs, Michigan

I hit up my old Entrepreneurship professor Jim Hunt. The one who said our GORUCK presentation was so great. He had a house in Harbor Springs, Michigan. We stopped through, jumped off his dock into the lake and said hello to his family when they came out of the house. Got a recommendation for The Fish Whisperer from a diner in town. Full of sundresses and ice cream cones here. America in all its innocence.

Dropped another cache, which his daughter recovered. Professor wasn't gonna make it in time to see us — we were on our way.

The finality of the trip, the states unvisited, having Java with me.

Let the world burn down, everyone can quit we'll be fine.

July 31st / Pere Marquette River, Baldwin, Michigan

The Fish Whisperer is a name some guy gave himself and then completely backed it up. He had a million lures and was happy to show us which ones were best for this time of year, and why. This one's what they're biting now because of the bugs. I thought of *A River Runs Through It*, one of my all time favorite books, and wished Brad Pitt didn't have to die.

Alex photographed him pulling a monster of a fish out of the river, catch and release, while I hung out with Java on the trails farther away so he wouldn't scare the fish. One of the nicest guys ever, I sent an email to my Dad that if he was looking for a fishing guide up here, I found his guy. The Fish Whisperer.

You guys can come fish with me anytime, he said as we were about to leave. Glad you got that shot, send it to me when you can.

August 1 / Chicago, IL / Rock'n'Roll Half Marathon

Alex and I were at the start point early. It was crowded, I had Java and my GR1.

We didn't talk about anything. My assumption was that we were gonna run together. He had something different in mind. He stuck with us after the gun went off, while the herd was still thick. Once he saw daylight, off he went and it was just me and Java.

Java was the only dog out there. I'm not even sure if dogs were allowed to run in this. We didn't register, we just showed up.

The cops smiled, the other runners smiled, they asked me all about Java. That's some dog you got there to run a half marathon. We stopped often, I poured water on his neck and gave him all the time he wanted. I was in no rush.

It was a beautiful day, this was the town that I had run my only marathon, with Emily. I drove from Fort Bragg to Chicago to run it with her and her girlfriend on no notice. I didn't want her to do it without me, so why not. I thought I was ready for it, but it crushed me. Our pace was 6 minutes/mile for the first 20 miles, then began the long limp to the finish. I remember fat people in spandex passing me at the end, and being really upset about it. How are they beating me, I thought. It was a shameful day, and I could barely bend either of my knees for the whole drive back as I thought about it.

Java and I were in no such rush. It took us forever. When we crossed the finish line, a woman put a medal around my neck, I said we did this and looked down at Java. She smiled hugely and gave me a second one.

I put it on Java's neck and gave him a big hug with everything I had while he licked the salt off my cheeks. I asked someone to take a picture of us while we waited to find Alex.

It was packed at the finish line, eventually he walked by. He asked me to take a picture of him to share with his girlfriend. I always loved his Romance tattoo above his heart. Told Emily a long time ago that if I had thought of that first, that's the tattoo I would have gotten.

We found the car, stopped at a gas station to fill up and pick up a couple hot dogs for Java. We drove out to the La Quinta by O'Hare Airport, and set our stuff down.

I went and bought a 12-pack of Budweiser and we both stared at our computers so we didn't have to talk about anything.

The next morning, I dropped him off at O'Hare and we said our goodbyes at the curb.

It was just me and Java now and I felt a million times better about everything.

And then there were two.

My dad loved Harleys,
so I loved Harleys.

August 2 / Milwaukee, Wisconsin / Harley Davidson Museum

Harley Davidson was always one of my favorite brands. I have these memories of my dad in his garage with his buddies, drinking Budweiser and working on their Harleys. Riding around Dayton on the back of his 1978 SuperGlide as a kid, one time Nana and Pa drove by the opposite direction on Dorothy Lane in front of the Dollar Theater and I could see my Nana's jaw hit the ground in the car. My mom told me later when I got home after that summer that I was to never ride on the back of a motorcycle ever again.

But there was also a business case on Harley Davidson in school that was my favorite. How the brand got too cheap, put their logo on everything. Lost their way trying to appeal to new people. There aren't enough people like my dad, I guess. I remember how much he loved Harley and still does, how you wave at a fellow Harley rider when you pass them on the road. If they have another bike, not so much. You park together downtown in the Oregon District. All the Harleys lined up, all the other bikes strewn about, somewhere else.

The museum had all sorts of cool old pictures and the first Harley Davidson behind some glass. Maybe someday GORUCK will have a museum and the first GR1 will be behind glass.

August 3 / Madison, Wisconsin

GQ said Context Clothing in Madison, Wisconsin was the third best small mens shop in the country. "Where New Brands Break First" it said. Parked by the capitol building, farmers market going on. They'd never let this happen in DC, too much security risk. Left Java in the truck, car running, doors locked. Walked a block and a half into Context Clothing. Vintage American flag, felt expensive in there.

Guy behind the counter said hello, recognized him from some of their pics online. Did a quick lap around the store, introduced myself. I'm Jason from a brand called GORUCK. Wondering if there's anyone I could talk to about our line of military-grade backpacks that we build in the USA.

Just as that happened a lady barged in the door, out of breath. We both turned to her, it was like Kramer from Seinfeld except more of a Janis Joplin look. "You!" and she pointed at me "You left your dog in your car, it's 100 degrees outside, you're going to kill him!"

I got the impression she was the pacifist type who would have no problem slitting my throat or anyone else's guilty of any crimes against animals. I looked at the guy behind the counter real quick, and started to smile as I reached into my pocket to pull out my remote key lock.

"Ma'am," and I showed her the key fob. "That dog is the great love of my life. We're traveling all over the country this summer, we've been to almost every state in the Lower 48 together. I have the A/C on full blast, he has plenty of water in the back of the truck. He's doing just fine."

Her eyes grew even wider with a different shocking kind of anger. She let out a deep loud breath and stormed back out without saying a word. I looked back at the guy behind the counter and he started laughing, I started laughing.

"Wow, she's something."

"Yeah, you can't make that up."

He chuckled, "We love dogs here."

"Cool, I wasn't sure. You mind if I go get him and bring him in?"

"Yeah, I'll go get Ryan, he's the owner and lead buyer."

Back to get Java, I also grabbed one of each of the rucks and our brand print-outs. I met Ryan, his vintage t-shirt probably cost $75, nice guy, big smile, easy going look. We went to the back corner of the shop, I told him face-to-face was always better, that I wanted to check out the shop in person and then see if we were a good fit. I thought of the vintage flag hanging up and thought, how are we not? I walked him through the rucks, the laptop compartment, the materials, why silent zippers are so important, told him I was in Special Forces, these were based on the rucks I had used there. Didn't mention Iraq, not that kind of town.

"Special Forces, huh? Cool."

"Yeah, they look nice. I'm thinking, great, do you want some I have a full SportRack full of them."

"Let me get with Sam, thanks a million for stopping in, stay in touch."

"Cool, thanks man."

Big smiles on both sides, and that was that.

August 4th / Minneapolis, MN

Boo-Boo's (Aunt Thea's) house just outside Minneapolis. Uncle Mike burned some steaks. Sleeping in a bed is nicer than sleeping in the truck.

10,000 lakes, Java found several of them.

Boo-boo had my Special Forces graduation picture in the guest room where I was staying. I don't even know if I have one of those. Those days feel like someone else's life. Weird to see it here, so out of place like a starship.

Cache at one of the lakes. Cracked phone. Uncle Mike got the cache.

August 6th / Fargo, ND

Drifter with the bike in front of the bike shop. So stress free, life on a bike seat. Sipping his coffee what's next who cares? Reminds me of heading to Europe in 2002 with no plan, just for something to do. Figure it out when you're there. He did some Zen karate shit at the end, who are you kidding man.

Big sign downtown FARGO super cool. Where was that in the movie? Bike shop just on the other side of the tracks. People are really friendly here, wonder if it's like that in the winter. Probably.

Big state, creek for Java before a lot of time on the road. Couple making out in the park, on the grass by the tennis courts. When he gets tired of chasing the stick, he sits down and starts gnawing on the stick. Makes me chase him, I throw the stick again, he barks and tries to keep it away from me. Truce ends back at the truck.

GETTING PULLED OVER, AGAIN.

"Were you just not paying attention or what?"

Another opportunity to make a friend in law enforcement.

80 in a 75. Consolation prize.

Thank you, Officer.

August 7 / North Dakota, Teddy Roosevelt National Park

Nobody in the parking lot, nice and dark. Up at first light, prairie dogs everywhere, Java whimpering to get out. Hope there aren't snakes. Run on the trail, off leash.

Back to the car, prairie dogs everywhere. Whack a mole, run here they disappear. Turn up there, run there. Same thing. Went on for an hour, smiling the whole time.

Target practice from the North to the South. Sturgis here we come.

North Dakota

August 7 / Sturgis

Biggest motorcycle rally in the world. Heard about it since forever. I've been a fan of Sturgis since forever, and have family and friends that have been riding there for years now. Sturgis is about a lot more than the small town of 6,000 or so, it's about the adventure of getting there and riding the open roads in the parks when you do. While the town itself is a necessary destination, the beauty of the event is in the Badlands, on a Harley, with friends alongside. August 9, 2010 is the first day of the 70th version, expected attendance 500,000, including us.

August 8 / Sturgis & Badlands, South Dakota

Wish I had a Harley. Sidecar for Java. Badlands is super underrated, not sure why everyone doesn't have this on the list of places to come to.

"Camping" in Custer State Park. Drove to the campsite, asked if there was a spot. Said it sold out a year ago. Next year was almost sold out already. Plenty of room in the truck, though, so that's good.

Crazy traffic. Buffalo blocking everything, donkeys too. Standstill for an hour. Herd of buffalo to our left. Java's going crazy. I get out of the car, run up the hill, buffalo in the background, thought Java might jump out of the window.

August 9 / Cody, WY / Cassie's, National Rodeo

Hadn't thought of my sister in a while. Big sign - Cassie's. Let's stop there. Former bootleg running whorehouse. Saloon dancing now. One guy straight out of the 1850's, Johnny Cash black, string tie. Another guy in some grey t-shirt that said Bahamas, white tube socks with short shorts. Ready for the cruise or whatever.

"Not responsible for women left overnite" said the sign above the dance floor. I always wanted to learn how to dance. Em was always more into salsa, don't think she ever took lessons but just had it. I was always embarrassed a little bit because at our wedding I didn't know how to really dance. Jack laughed at me, said I had no rhythm, no style. It was funny, you can write off anything on your wedding day, it'll all be OK we're in love.

Happily ever after.

Not that hungry, the rest of the steak for Java. Rodeo. Those bulls are enormous. People think Special Forces is dangerous. Bull Riding is insane.

You're guaranteed to fall then some clown tries to distract the bull so he doesn't crush your skull.

August 10 / Yellowstone

Didn't even ask about the campsites. More buffalo, everywhere. Too many cars, feel like cattle. Trailhead, wander off. Hope we don't see any bears.

Enormous skies, huge lakes. Clean air, clear water. Lots of swimming. Drying Java off, that spot under his neck and his back leg starts to kick.

Back to traffic.

Then to open roads.

I miss you, Scott

August 11 / Big Fork, Montana

"The Last Best Place"

R.I.P. Scott. Six years since Scott died.

My best friend in the Army, we were supposed to go through all the training together, life was supposed to work out differently. I didn't see his death coming. Crying at his funeral with our drill sergeant. Missing his funeral because I had more training left to go. Hugging his parents in General Lambert's office when they pulled me out of the field. Here he is, ashes to ashes dust to dust. I feel cold and angry, then the tears, the emotion come back. The picture that Emily took at our graduation is the picture his parents use for the Foundation they set up in his name.

Rode in Scott's old white Ford Explorer, the one he had at Fort Bragg, that I helped him pick out, went to a Montana-style steak and beer joint with his parents. Didn't disappoint.

Scott's dad sees Scott when he looks at me. I wish I could go back in time and bring him back and do so many other things too.

August 12 / Idaho, Coeur d'Alene

Potatoes are the thing here. Idaho potatoes, best around. Best burger in town, the Wall Street Journal said, Hudson Hamburgers. Countertop kind of place, super crowded. Don't serve fries. Mystery to me. But hey we're here. One for me, one for Java. It's good. Would have been better with fries. They probably could do a lot more business that way, too. Add a few bucks to almost every order, that kind of stuff adds up.

August 12 / Seattle, Washington / Space Needle

Feels like check-in at a hotel, valet and cars coming and going. Park and get out, steal a picture of Java underneath, proof of the visit, off we go.

Stopped by Blackbird. Kind of like Context but less friendly. Empty store, cold and perfect. Gave my card and left the packet to a guy in rolled-up black jeans who wasn't interested in talking about anything since I wasn't buying. Said email was the best way to get in touch, Nicole is the owner/buyer, not there right now. Maybe she's nicer. Probably threw my stuff in the trash. Need to reach out next week.

Shit sleep next to the train tracks. Coffee from the original Starbucks at Pike Place Market. Hit the road.

47 states down. One more to go.

Best pic of the Space Needle, ever

August 13 / Portland, Oregon / Bagdad Cafe

48th State of the GORUCK Summer.

People shitting in parks downtown. Feral dogs everywhere. Shopping carts full of trash, and cans.

Gorgeous day, bright blue skies.

Bagdad Cafe, across the river. Looked like a theater, people sitting outside. Nicer part of town. Let's grab a beer, Java. Just me and Java, people walking by, cars come, cars go. I'll take something light, a wheat beer or whatever. 48th state, we did it. This is our victory beer, Java.

Nobody was there to meet us, or greet us. Nobody to call, nothing to do that mattered at all. Just drink your beer. Rub Java's ears.

More cars come and go, more people walking by. The world comes and the world goes. It's not a bad place to drink a beer.

Baghdad used to be such a nice place, they said. Now it's a warzone, Sadr City is one of the worst places on planet earth. Feral dogs, people shitting everywhere there too. Lots more guns, though. And they hate Americans. Fuck them.

This is living, a beer on an outdoor patio with Java.

==At the Bagdad Cafe that doesn't remind me of Baghdad at all.==

Not a care in the world, just a beer and a dog and nobody trying to kill me.

Here we are, Java, we did it.

August 14 / Off The Grid / Oregon

Leslie's brother Chris. No cell phone, doesn't trust the government. Thinks the end of the world is coming soon. Lives in the mountains. Met at Walmart parking lot, said I wouldn't be able to find his place from Google Maps, I have to follow him.

Windy dirt roads leading up.

Solar panels, vegetable gardens, beers from WalMart, a hose shower, some woodwork in progress. Seems happy, good for him. Could be fun to do for a while, not sure about forever. Hope the end of days doesn't come anytime soon.

Driving through the Redwoods, we felt really, really small. And yet we kept on, staring into fog and all of the above, enjoying the scenery when we could, and always the anonymity of insignificance when compared to Nature.

Stayed at Cassie's empty apartment in Humboldt. Smells like a dope depository, ==if I had to pass a drug test I'd fail just from breathing in this place.== Almost slept in the car. Smiled thinking about that time she flew home with pot brownies in her checked luggage, then our dog George ate them all when we were at Christmas Eve Service. Had to rush him to the hospital, charcoal all over his fur, pumped his stomach. Fun Christmas, sucked to be her. She's lucky she's not in prison still to this day.

Cool night, left the window open. Snuggled with Java to stay warm under the covers.

August 15 / San Francisco, California / Outside Lands

Dropped Java off with Frieder and his family in Marin. Headed to Golden Gate Park. Picked Cassie and Amy up at their hotel.

Al Green, Phoenix, Kings of Leon. Snuck my big camera in, slung under my t-shirt and my Jacket. Peace and love is the vibe. Love songs go great with that.

Summer concerts were always such a thing with my dad. I'd show up at the airport, he'd show me the tickets he'd bought for us to go to that year. Don Henley, Riverbend in Cincy was my first. We had tickets to see the Grateful Dead, but then Jerry died. Sad day.

Two kids eating a sandwich between sets. One had an American flag draped over his forearm. I wondered if he was going to drop it, it made me nervous how he was barely holding it. How about fold it up right, asshole, that's what I was thinking. What would I do if he dropped it? I'd have to say something. What if he told me to go fuck myself? I could feel the rage building. Didn't really want to spend the night in jail, wanted to get back to Java. I took my picture and walked away. Never saw them again.

Phoenix set was one of the best I've ever heard - crowd-surfing!

Left halfway through Kings of Leon, wasn't feeling it.

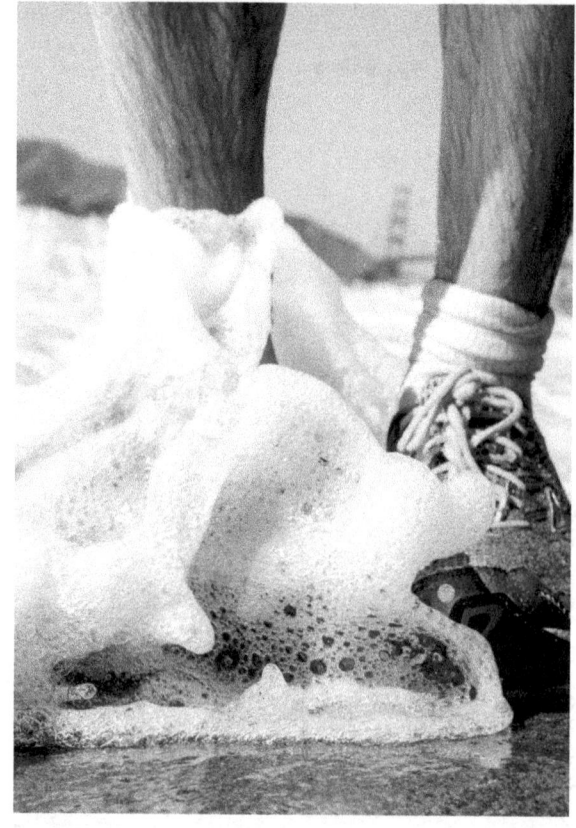

August 17 / San Francisco, CA / Route Recon / GORUCK Challenge

Finalized the plan with Tough Mudder. Their next event was at Lake Tahoe, so the first ever GORUCK Challenge would be in San Francisco a couple weeks prior. September 25th. Had to figure out what to do, what the route would be. Where can I park? Went to the beach, just by Golden Gate Park. Good start point. Ran the trail north with Java. Plenty of good places to do other stuff and take cool pictures.

The blog post I published:

The route is set for the GORUCK Challenge in San Fran. Ocean running, stairs, natural obstacle courses, city running through billions in real estate and the big bridge in the background of wet shoes all play an important part. Oh yeah, and Zeitgeist downtown the night before for some ruckoff camaraderie. It's meant to be fun and tough, a challenge for adventure seekers to share, together, and experience some good livin' in the process.

I wanted to get some perfect picture of my shoes getting all wet, the waves crashing. Bent over, got the Golden Gate Bridge in the background. Wave crashed alright. Got my camera, too. Fade to black.

Time to drive back to DC.

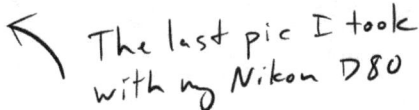

The last pic I took with my Nikon D80

GORUCK Truck - For sale

Thankfully nobody bought it.

Epilogue

From: Emily <█████████████>
Date: Fri, Sep 10, 2010 at 7:09 AM
Subject: tone = sad, not accusatory (read at own peril)
To: Jason J. McCarthy <████████@gmail.com>

i just woke up to a bad dream.

i remember most of it, i was graduating from georgetown but there was no pomp/circumstance.

i was waiting in a long line to get my transcript, 160 credits required to graduate. there were problems printing my transcript, i waited and waited and waited only to be handed a shoddy print job on ripped fax paper.

but the most upsetting part was that i only had 137 credits for some reason. no one told me i was short. now i would have to take additional classes in order to truly graduate. but it went on from there.

i was thinking in a dream state about you.

i was wondering why my sacrifices and out-of-body living for so long didn't merit some sort of compensation.

i wondered why you didn't fight for me when i needed your love most. last november was a pivotal month, in retrospect and i think even then.

i wondered how it could have gone so wrong. i don't have selective short term memory.

i remember how exhausting it was for us both.

i remember how stubborn i was being and the safeguards i was holding onto because i was scared to jump again into your arms. but i believed then and still do to this day that i had already jumped in, full force, and i felt that i had been left to drown.

the delicious irony in all this, is that deep down, i feel rejected. i know that you do too, we both can and were.

there were always limits on your love, perhaps risk-calculating ones, based in logic, but there were limits. i built my life to try to make you proud, got caught up in unsafe territory and came to feel more betrayed and lost.

i acknowledge and respect the suffering you have gone through as a result of me.

the guilt still lives in my heart and visits me everyday. you know why i left and anyone who knows me sees the power you possess over me that, power that knows no equal.

this isn't the first time i've asked myself why you let me go.

are you happier without me?

did you decide that i wasn't worthy of you after all?

had you had enough?

what changed it for you?

why wouldn't you do what it would take to get me to stay?

i was there, with you, and you would only go so far. and would it have been worth it, after all, would it have been worth while, after the sunsets and the dooryards and the sprinkled streets, after the novels, after the teacups, after the skirts that trail along the floor and this, and so much more?

From: Jason McCarthy <████████@gmail.com>
Date: Sat, Sep 11, 2010 at 1:39 AM
Subject: Re: tone = sad, not accusatory (read at own peril)
To: Emily <████████████>

... It is impossible to say just what I mean! And yet it seems appropriate for me, too, to quote from my favorite poem of a guy so paralyzed that he questioned "do I dare to eat a peach". It's like, just eat the damn peach and then go for your walk on the beach with the mermaids singing each to each. Mermaids don't have to sing to you...

Of course you knew to quote prufrock with me :)

Em, for the life of me i don't know what happened with me, with you, with us, with life, with the whole thing.

i still don't, but it seems surreal and not quite right. i wasn't me, i'm not me, and you weren't you, and aren't you.

it's not the way i wanted life to be, and not the way i want life to be.

it seems like you want to reach out to me, to be heard. it's hard to talk about this stuff, i'm really hard to talk to on some levels, but not so much on others (bff).

i'm here to say that i hear you, and thank you for talking to me, and that i really hear you.

i read your note over and over and i hear sadness, i hear regret, and i hear you saying that you're so, so sorry for all that you did, for the 50% of our failed marriage that you were responsible for.

I also hear you saying that life doesn't make sense to you right now. That life has a mind of its own, that it feels surreal to you, that you don't know how you got where you are now, that you fought for us for so long, that you have nothing to show for it now, and that the failure attached to it has cast a really negative light over the fact that you tried, for so long, to the best you could, to make me proud and do everything in your power to do what you, and we, thought was best for us.

But now it seems like the failure has overshadowed all of the years of waiting, all of your sacrifices. And as life has gone as it has gone, and our paths forked, i hear you wondering, as i do, how it happened, and i hear frustration in the answer, or lack thereof.

i also hear you expressing the fact that i have a power over you like none other, that given this power i should have been able to convince you to stay with me.

That I should not have let you leave.

I also hear torn feelings about where you are now, how can you start over but not start over? At least with ice cream, there's tomorrow, and a full appetite, right? With me, with life, with where you are now, it seems much more difficult, the choices you feel you have to make, and are asked to make, much more difficult and somehow much more serious. And paralyzingly tough, and I hear the lament at the years that have gone by.

I hear your pain, I hear the sadness of loss, the sadness of grief, and the attempt to really try your hardest to move forward. And the failure to do that. And yet this is me, so I also hear you.

I hear the Em I knew, and know, buried a little deeper, but I hear her. Em, I'll always hear you. And as I mentioned, you're gonna get you back. I promise. And I hear your love for me, for the promise of us, for the regret of us, for the idea that we will always love each other, and have a power over each other unique in this world.

You are right to think, and say, that nobody will ever know me as you do.

As for your specific questions, the answers seem like graveyards, though graveyards I wish were not. Your present situation, how you've moved away and moved on makes me want to cocoon myself away, drink my 6 pack alone at night, walk around anonymously, and rub Java's belly first thing every morning to rave reviews from one chocolate mutt.

Failure, rejection etc. some of the themes you hit on.

But what's hard is that you are currently engaged to be married, a promise of commitment I respect. I don't know him, at all, as in zero, but part of the answers of why I didn't this or couldn't do that, or use my power, tie into the fact that this has been going on for a long while, and this is the source of my paralysis. I say this not to accuse or point fingers, but to explain why I was not always able to give enough.

I think I felt it was for you to convince me that you at least wanted to focus on us, without such distractions. I really don't say this to make you feel bad, I'm still caught up in explanation, which perhaps is the graveyard I should let lie in peace.

So what if in the middle came all the indecision, the visions and revisions, the do i dare's and the trousers rolled, the mermaids singing each to each, what if it read simply, let us go then, you and I, till human voices wake us, and we drown. And the rest of the world can burn for all I care?

All the rest of your questions seem more like small steps taken forward than questions, and i know they are hard to ask for fear of the answers.

But what if after all that we had been through that was exactly the way it had to be, at that time, given who and where we were, and damn the world's peering eyes, and what if the 'this, and so much more' were just a brief portion of the path, what if the sense we both sought is actually still staring us in the face?

what if we were wrong, and right, all at the same time?

What if the fax paper was just a silly mistake, a crinkled and rolled-up illegible piece of paper from a past, into a future where fax paper doesn't exist anymore and apologies carry the weight that they warrant.

What if we were both right. And if we were both wrong.

And what if we really had the courage to say who cares?

Where do you think that would take us?

From: Emily <██████████████>
Date: Sat, Sep 11, 2010 at 2:39 PM
Subject: loading dock
To: Jason McCarthy <███████@gmail.com>

jase, i received your message last night as i stood on the curb of the bolles school, the exact spot where you asked me almost 16 years ago to the day if i needed a ride to the atp. the cross-country bus from tampa arrived a little after 2 am. i sat for a long time in my car in the parking lot, came home and didn't fall asleep until the time when most people get up.

i think i'm mostly speechless from what you wrote. as the day went on yesterday, i realized, i feared and then i resigned myself to the harsh reality that i had wrote you spuriously and selfishly and was afraid to even reread it, and that you were probably going to either ignore or berate or misunderstand what i was trying to say.

it seems that you did none of those things. you heard me, i think for the first time in a long while, but you heard me even better than i heard myself in many ways.

since then, i've been floating in a mixture of relief and uncertainty and hope and regret; just the right ingredients for further paralysis, at least for now.

i'm writing you to tell you i'm still thinking and need a little time to write back a response. you raised a lot of questions that i wasn't expecting to be there.

you heard a lot of things i've been trying to hear within myself.

i'll get back to you soon to continue the conversation.

♡

Sometimes it works out exactly like it's supposed to

emily & jason
Part Deux
July 29, 2017

I had thought to end it on Em's email, a cliffhanger of sorts.

Your imagination could run wild with all the foreshadowing — the GORUCK Challenge was an overnight success, the business started printing money, Emily met me in DC right after the summer and we got back together, and Java lived forever. Those are the next chapters, right?

Well, not exactly.

The decade built on top of all this rubble feels worthy of its own explanation, the 'how to' part of the GORUCK story I am living now but not writing about, mostly because it's still live action.

Emily persuaded me after reading these pages that this isn't really the GORUCK story at all, it's much more than that and I shouldn't be so arcane. Wrap it up a little bit, she said, it's OK if someone smiles at the end. And she's right, so here we are.

But, hardest things first.

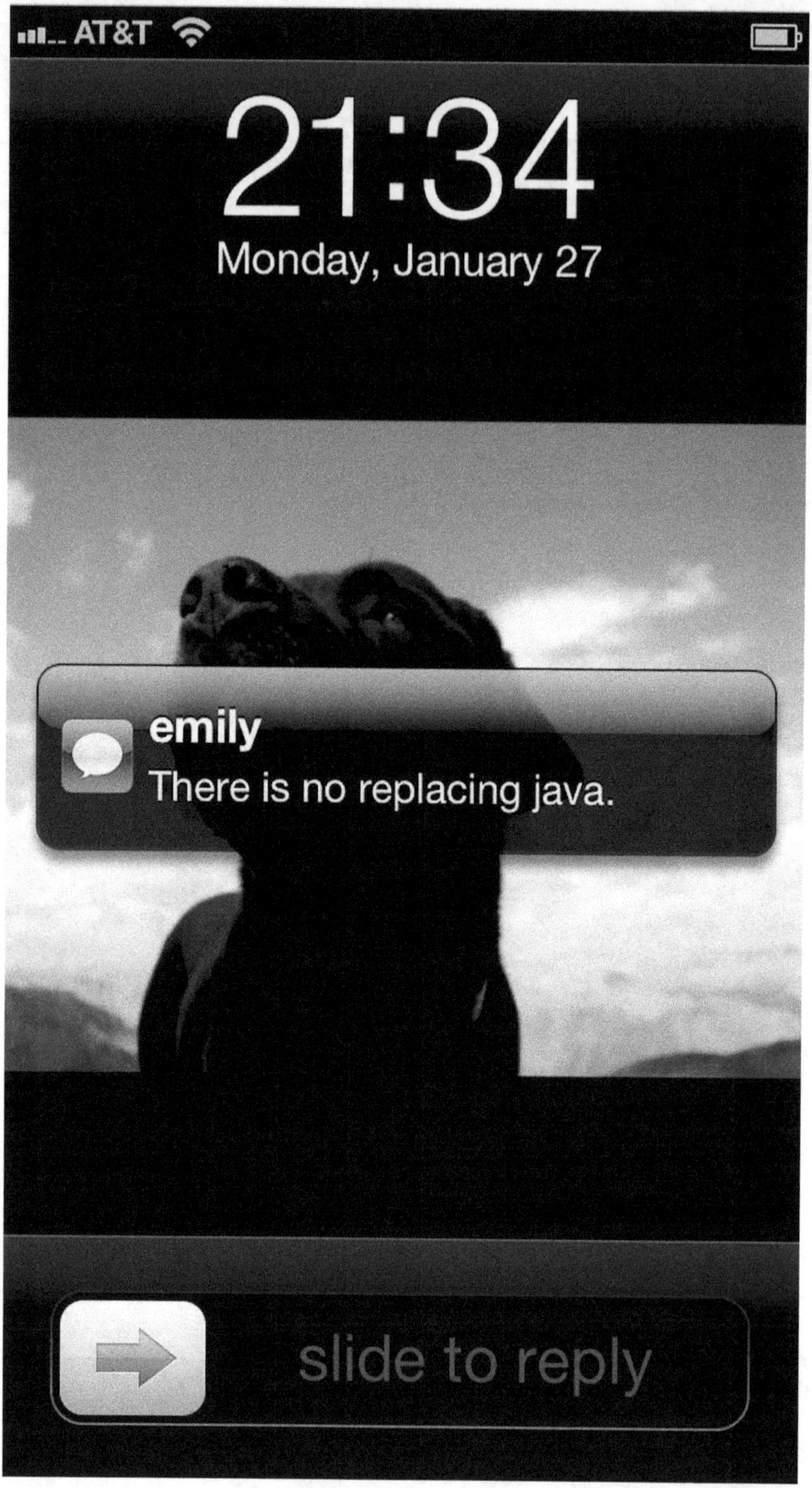
AT&T
21:34
Monday, January 27
emily
There is no replacing java.
slide to reply

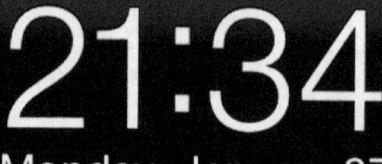

In 2013, Java got some sort of auto-immune disease.

I watched his body eat away at itself, day after day, at a hospital outside DC. His stress levels were so high the first night without me there that the Doctor broke policy and allowed me to stay overnight from that point on. Much of my time was spent curled up on the hard floor next to Java, we fought for his life, together. He didn't have to go through any of it alone.

Emily heard Java's last breath because I called her, and he got to hear her voice for the last time as I held him with all my heart. It was four days after his seventh birthday. His ashes rest on my desk at work, in a big awesome top-of-the-line walnut urn that I bought right after he passed. I can't bring myself to part with them yet, I'm still not ready to say a final goodbye, even all these years later. Deep down I know that the ocean calls us one last time.

Remembering the story, like that, gets me every time. So no, Java didn't live forever. But we did start a non-profit called Java Forever that evolved into the GORUCK Foundation. We focus on Veteran issues and physical fitness and raise a bunch of money to that end. Out of tragedy comes a call to do good, it's up to each of us how we answer that.

Class 001

The Business of GORUCK

How Not To Start a Backpack Company is kind of a joke, the title makes me laugh. The last thing the world needed, and this still holds true, is another backpack company. I never wanted to start a backpack company, GORUCK has never acted like a backpack company, and it will never be a backpack company as long as I'm around.

But that doesn't mean I knew exactly how that could, or would work out.

My first plan was to drive around the country and talk about America and you saw how that turned out. When Java and I finished the route recon for The GORUCK Challenge, I had no idea that these events would forever alter the course of our lives.

On September 25, 2010 at Class 001 in San Francisco, GORUCK transformed from a gear company to a people-first brand. We planted our flag on the high ground, and it was an open invitation to anyone out there to come and test yourself at this really challenging adventure based on Special Forces training, led by Green Berets. The people who showed up became all the proof I needed that the human spirit is alive and well all across America, not just in the military. And that gave me the strength to take that retail growth plan that my business school professors liked so much, and throw it out the window.

My second year at business school I felt like Tyler Durden in Fight Club. Traveling somewhere new every weekend, leading back-to-back 12-hour Challenges. 50+ miles a weekend. Taking the subway to the airport for my flight home, drooling on my hoodie before we even take off, landing with blood shot eyes, heading to Jill and Tony's house up by the National Cathedral to be reunited with Java, and for a home-cooked dinner they insisted I eat before passing out. I mention their names as a reminder that a lot of people helped me along the way and there's no shame in that, ever.

The highs that people felt after finishing the Challenge, after doing this really hard thing together - those were the highs I was searching for, too. I found it weekend after weekend by passing on some of what I had learned in Special Forces. Then the finishers told all their friends about GORUCK. The new first rule of Fight Club was, tell everyone about Fight Club. Some of these friends signed up for the Challenge, a lot started buying the gear.

So, the chronology of sorts — GORUCK started with the gear, created the events to help market the gear, the events became our focus because that's where our heart is (with people), and the people who took our events started forming their own communities and doing it under the banner of GORUCK. Awareness went from nothing to a lot more than that, and the

community spread the word for us.

A decade later, we lead over 1,000 events a year and have over 300 GORUCK Clubs all over the world. Thousands of people have gotten GORUCK tattoos. One guy even used a cattle brand. Yes, on himself.

It's a different way to build a business, but it's textbook community building — the exact playbook of the Green Berets that I had learned and lived and was applying intuitively, and not intentionally. You work by, with, and through a local partner force, you advise and assist them (aka leadership) and they do the work for you to achieve your desired end state. They're your force multipliers.

That's how GORUCK has been built one person at a time, and why the community is so strong.

I owe this way of life to the Special Forces community — without them, there would be no GORUCK. This is not a path you'll find by increasing your ad budget or hiring a slick marketing agency promising you easy money.

It's hard work, day after day. But it's worth our time investment because we love our people and we're proud members of our own community.

Emily

I hear her voice in every page of this story. She has always been my muse, and the love of my life. And in every way, she's the reason this book exists. When I said that I stumbled upon an old journal, that was the truth. But she stumbled across it first. She was looking for an old picture of Java in the GORUCK Truck to put on our Christmas card, next to the picture of our family now in the same GORUCK Truck. She stayed up all night to read it and told me in the morning that this was the story I should tell. Sort of how when we were in Abidjan she told me, "jase, you should do the GORUCK thing." And here we are.

So how did we get back together, you might wonder.

It's a fair question, really.

She had moved back home with her daughter Natalie around the same time that Java and I moved GORUCK back home to Florida. Unless you believe in star-crossed lovers, it was just a coincidence that we were both back in Florida at the same time. I was living on the beach in an appropriately dubbed 'Team House' with five other Special Forces guys, spending all the time I could find and then some on GORUCK. Java was still crashing the biggest waves with the best of them, and he was no stranger to long rucks by my side. I had accepted my life, and I loved it.

Java and I met Emily and Natalie (for the first time) at an outside courtyard restaurant just up the road. I had asked for her help planning a new urban survival event, cloak and dagger style. She said of course she'd meet up. I also asked if I could take a few pics of her wearing the Echo for our site. Sure, no problem, she said.

You see, people, there's always an excuse to get in touch.

After we chatted about the event, she put the ruck on and we walked out toward the beach. The weather was overcast with dark clouds on the horizon. It was about to open up so I said, OK stop right there, and you could see the path extend in the distance. I grabbed Natalie from Em and held her in my left arm. I was holding onto Java's leash, too, while I used my right hand to hold the big fancy camera and take pictures on burst. Java started barking like crazy, lunging toward some cat; Natalie started giggling, and Emily turned her head to the right to look over. I could see her smiling. It's all there for me in that picture. I can still remember what it felt like in that exact moment, how something so complicated could feel so casual, as if nothing had ever changed and this exact moment was our new life.

Then the heavens opened. We all ran through the downpour to Em's car, she loaded Nat up and drove home. I waved good-bye and rucked home

375

Monster
President, GORUCK Nation

with Java by my side, in the rain.

It's a hell of a thing to fall back in love, to remember the past but not dwell on it. To forgive them and for them to forgive you. To choose to spend a lifetime together, again. The falling back in love part happened fast — but trusting that new love took some time.

Emily started teaching in town but I kept asking her to work more on GORUCK stuff. First here and there, and then full-time. Distance might make the heart grow fond, but the trust we had to rebuild came from the time we would spend together. And yet she had a daughter and I had a company. It was easy to keep our guards up just by doing what needed to be done, day after day. Inertia can be one of life's greatest enemies.

Java remained our link. He loved us both unconditionally, never brought up the past, and we loved him for it. When he passed away, it brought us closer together. Nobody loved him like we did, Emily was the person I most wanted to cry with. And when I just wasn't myself for a little too long, she took it upon herself to get me another dog. I wasn't sure if I was ready, but she wasn't asking.

His name is Monster, he's from a small town in southern Ohio just like me. We gave him the title of President, GORUCK Nation, and he's the reason our kids aren't scared of 'monsters'.

Emily is responsible for all that's best in my life, and their names are Natalie, Jack, and Ryan. Natalie visits her dad when she has breaks from school, just like I visited my dad in Ohio when I was a kid. She loves paint, chalk, crayons, cardboard, string and tape. She refuses help of any kind while working on her next masterpiece. She believes that tracing is a form of cheating, and art thieves like her brothers prize her creations for their absolute originality.

Jack and Ryan conspire with impunity, mount revolutions multiple times a day, and possess sorcerer's magic to turn into alligators, cheetahs, dragons, and any other creature they can imagine. They defy evil and villainous parents who try to do horrible things like get them to school on time. Mornings at our house remind me of those National Geographic specials with the wrestling lion cubs, and the day escalates from there. We got exactly the kids we deserve.

This journey Emily and I are on together is beautiful not for its perfection, but for its scars. And because it's ours.

It's hard to chase your dreams, it's hard to fail at the most important things in life, it's hard to pick yourself back up again, and again, and again. It's hard to ask for help, to make yourself vulnerable.

It's hard to say I'm sorry. It's hard for you, and for me, and for Emily. It's hard for all of us.

But it's better together.

Dreaming big dreams is worth it. It's OK to learn as we go, to make mistakes and to repent however we have to, or need to.

The hardest parts just might be the prequel to the best that's yet to come. We'll never know unless we keep dreaming and keep chasing them down with all we got. God bless anyone who dares so greatly.

I hate good-byes, but this isn't the end.

To echo Em, I'll get back to you soon to continue the conversation.

Our family ♡

The GORUCK Truck
2019

A Note About The Author

Jason McCarthy is the Founder and CEO of GORUCK. He served with 10th Special Forces Group in Iraq and West Africa from 2006-08 and now lives in Jacksonville Beach, Florida with his family. He proudly serves on the Board of Directors of the Green Beret Foundation.

use your camera phone

We'd love to hear from you

CPSIA information can be obtained
at www.ICGtesting.com
Printed in the USA
LVHW012124220820
663909LV00002B/2